THE
New York
Giants
Trivia Book:
Revised and
Updated

THE
New York Giants Trivia Book:
Revised and Updated

Michael Lichtenstein

ST. MARTIN'S GRIFFIN
NEW YORK

www.stmartins.com

Library of Congress Cataloging-in-Publication Data

Lichtenstein, Michael.
   The New York Giants trivia book : revised and updated/Michael Lichtenstein.
      p.   cm.
   ISBN 0-312-28664-3
   1. New York Giants (Football team)—Miscellanea.   I. Title.

GV956.N4 L53 2001
796.332'64'097471—dc21

2001031817

First Edition: September 2001

10 9 8 7 6 5 4 3 2 1

For Marty Glickman
1917–2001

ACKNOWLEDGMENTS

I want to thank the following people for their support and friendship in writing this book. Steve Shestakofsky, who always knew Jim Podoley was the "secret weapon" in 1961. Also, I'd like to thank Jerry Pinkus for his fine photos and Doug Murphy and the New York Giants for their cooperation with this book. My Monday morning quarterback club of Michael Anderson and Dave Kelly; my marine buddies Ed McDowell—a good writer in his own right—and Ray Wrigley; Tony Mendillo, the biggest Giant fan I know; Nancy Martinez-Ruiz just for being the person she is; and my St. Martin's family of Marc Resnick and Joe Rinaldi.

CONTENTS

INTRODUCTION

Reading this book is like perusing a family album. So many wonderful memories! So many true and lasting football heroes!

As a schoolboy in Brooklyn, I had seen the Giants play against the Brooklyn Dodgers at Ebbets Field. (Yes, Brooklyn had a fine NFL team in the 1930s.) I watched Benny Friedman, Mel Hein, Jim Lee Howell, Harry Newman, Ken Strong, and so many of the great old-timers of two-way football. Did you know that I played for the Giants? Well, it was the Jersey City Giants, the farm team for the New York Giants coached by Bill Owen, Steve Owen's brother. I wasn't good enough for the big club, but we did use the Giants A formation and we trained with the New York club. Playing both ways, I was the tailback and signal caller on offense and the safety man in the 6-2-2-1 defense. Merely mentioning those football phrases sends my memory racing back.

That's what this book is all about . . . the good old days. Of course the modern stars like Phil Simms and Lawrence Taylor are in it, too, but for me, those marvelous moments and great players of long ago are especially captivating.

Emlen Tunnell, running back punts at the Polo Grounds; Arnie Weinmeister, number 73, the only number visible in a sea of mud as he had not been on his back all game; Al Blozis, killed in action in World War II only months after wearing a Giants uniform; the day Y. A. Tittle threw seven touchdown passes at Yankee Stadium to tie Sid Luckman's 1943 NFL record; Ken Strong, kicking field goals and points-after; "That's all, brother"; Frank Gifford making all-pro his rookie year as a defensive back while playing offense and defense; the willowy grace of Del Shofner; "the best football game ever played"; the rise to football glory of Phil Simms; Lawrence Taylor's greatest game; Al DeRogatis readjusting his displaced kneecap as he sat on the turf between plays—again and again; and Mel Hein, Eddie Price, Joe Morrison, Kyle Rote, John Cannady, "Tuffy" Leemans, Ward Cuff, Ed

Danowski, Bull Karcis, "Feets" Barnum, Hank Soar, Tom Landry . . . we were in awe of all of them.

The feeling I remember best of all was the joy they took in playing and being together and in projecting that fun and excitement to us.

That's what this book by Michael Lichtenstein is all about—the nostalgia of joy experienced by any football fan, particularly the Giants fan. I commend it to you.

Marty Glickman
April 1995

1

THE EARLY YEARS: 1925–55

Questions:

1. What year was the Giants' inaugural season?

2. The Giants lost the first game in their existence, 14–0. Who was the opponent? a. The Chicago Bears b. The Green Bay Packers c. The Washington Redskins d. The Providence Steam Roller

3. What was the price Tim Mara paid for his NFL franchise, later to be called the Giants?

4. What was Tim Mara's profession?

5. Who was the Giants' first head coach? He had been a college coach for a number of years, most notably at Navy.

6. Who was the Giants' marquee player in their maiden season?

7. In the kickoff season, more than 70,000 fans filled the Polo Grounds for the final game that year. The Giants had been running in the red going into that game, but the huge ticket sales turned the franchise around, and the Giants ended the season in the black. They played the Chicago Bears, who that day featured what legendary all-American halfback from Illinois?

8. When did the Giants appear in their first NFL championship game? a. 1929 b. 1933 c. 1937 d. 1939

9. What game was known as the Sneakers Game?

10. From 1933 through 1945, the Giants appeared in how many championship games? a. 7 b. 3 c. 4 d. 9

11. Who was the Hall of Fame center who anchored the Giants line from 1931 to 1945?

12. Who was the Giants tackle of the late 1920s enshrined in both the NFL Hall of Fame and the Baseball Hall of Fame?

13. During their first twenty seasons, how many league championships did the Giants win? a. 6   b. 1   c. 3   d. 2

14. Who was the standout Giants tackle killed in action during World War II?

15. Which member of the 1941 Giants was presented the Congressional Medal of Honor for heroism in World War II? a. Hank Soar b. Ward Cuff c. Jack Lummus d. Frank Reagan

16. Who played end for the Giants in the 1930s and 1940s and would later be the Giants head coach in the 1950s? a. Will Walls b. Jim Lee Howell c. Vince Dennery d. Ray Poole

17. Who was the native New Yorker who was given a "day" by the Giants at the Polo Grounds in 1943 and then went on to throw seven touchdown passes against the Giants that day? a. Allie Sherman b. Tony Bova c. Sid Luckman d. George Cafego

18. Who coached the Giants from 1931 to 1953?

19. Who was the Giants top rusher of the late 1930s from Oregon? a. Kink Richards b. Red Wolfe c. Alphonse "Tuffy" Leemans d. Bull Karcis

20. Who was the all-around back who led the Giants in scoring from 1937 to 1942? a. Dale Burnett b. Ward Cuff c. Andy Marefos d. Jim Neill

21. Who was the first player selected by the Giants in the initial NFL draft?

22. Who was the Hall of Famer from New York University best known for his kicking in the 1930s and 1940s?

23. Which team were the Giants playing against on December 7, 1941, at the Polo Grounds? a. The Brooklyn Dodgers b. The Philadelphia Eagles c. The Detroit Lions d. The Cleveland Rams

24. Who is the winningest coach in Giants history? a. Allie Sherman b. Bill Parcells c. Steve Owen d. Tim Mara

25. Who was the first African American to play for the Giants?

26. Name the two Giants players from the 1946 team who were suspended from league play for associating with gamblers and failing to report a bribe prior to the NFL title game.

27. True or False: Steve Owen is credited with designing the Umbrella Defense.

28. Name the rookie quarterback acquired from the Redskins in 1948.

29. Who was the Giants assistant coach from the 1950s who would later be the winning head coach in the first two Super Bowls?

30. Match the player with his alma mater:

Charlie Conerly   Texas

Eddie Price   Penn State

Tom Landry   Duke

Roosevelt Grier   Mississippi

Al DeRogatis   Tulane

31. Who was the Columbia University end who led the Giants in receiving from 1948 to 1950? a. Bob McChesney b. Bill Swiacki c. Ellery Williams d. Kelley Mote

32. What year did the Giants select Frank Gifford in the NFL draft?

33. Who holds the record for the longest run from scrimmage by a New York Giant?

34. Which Giants running back ran for 218 yards against the Chicago Cardinals in a game during the 1950 season? a. Gene "Choo-Choo" Roberts b. Kyle Rote c. Frank Gifford d. Eddie Price

35. Who was known as Automatic Ben?

36. Which team was defensive star Andy Robustelli acquired from? a. The Los Angeles Rams b. The Chicago Cardinals c. The Pittsburgh Steelers d. The Brooklyn Dodgers

37. Which Giants defender led the NFL in interceptions in 1951 with 11?

38. Name the Giants kicker who had only one toe on his kicking foot.

39. Name the four-time All-Pro Giants defensive lineman from the early 1950s.

40. Which Giants defensive player served as a player-coach during the 1954 and 1955 seasons? a. Dick Nolan b. Tom Landry c. Pete Mangum d. Emlen Tunnell

41. Who replaced Steve Owen as Giants head coach in 1954?

42. Name the running back who joined the Giants in 1955 from the Canadian Football League.

43. Which Giants defensive lineman from the 1950s and 1960s went on to become an actor, singer, and minister?

44. Who was the unheralded late-round draft choice from Morgan State University who moved in as a starting offensive tackle in 1953 and would end up in the Hall of Fame?

45. Who was the all-American halfback from Southern Methodist University that the Giants converted to wide receiver? a. Forrest Griffith b. Bob Jackson c. Clarence Avinger d. Kyle Rote

"An Empty Store with Chairs in It"

The Legacy lives on: Wellington Mara, son of Giants founder Tim Mara. (Jerry Pinkus)

The year was 1925, the height of the roaring twenties, and Tim Mara was definitely a man about town. He was a successful businessman and bookie (bookmaking was legal during this time) who could count among his friends, if not customers, New York governor Al Smith and New York City mayor Jimmy Walker. Another friend, Billy Gibson, was the manager of heavyweight boxing champion Gene Tunney. Tim Mara wanted to invest in the pugilistic legend, but his contact with Gibson would take his business ventures into uncharted waters. Gibson was conferring with two gentlemen, one being NFL commissioner Joe Carr, about putting New

York on the NFL map. Carr wanted Gibson to put up the money for this new franchise, but Gibson was wary of this venture. Instead, he suggested his friend, Tim Mara, as a possible owner. Mara had never seen a football game in his life, but like any businessman, he asked the price. It was right, and a deal was made. The New York Giants were born.

To this day the actual price of purchasing the franchise is still in question. The figure has ranged from $500 to as much as $2,500, but according to Tim Mara's son, Wellington, when told the price, his father responded, "An empty store with chairs in it is worth that much in New York City."

Despite the warnings from his friend Al Smith that pro football would never make it, Tim Mara hung on to the Giants. That first season Smith's gloomy forecast seemed prophetic until the final home game of the season. The Giants had been running in the red, but the Chicago Bears came to town with the man who could put fans in the stands: Red Grange. More than 70,000 attended that game alone, which was enough to help the Giants finish in the black. Pro football had a toehold in New York.

Tim Mara died in 1959. He lived long enough to see his venture turn into one of the showcase franchises in all professional sports. In 1963 he was inducted into the National Football League Hall of Fame—as a charter member.

A Real Giant Hero

Al Blozis. (Georgetown University)

The winds of war were sweeping the world when Al Blozis graduated from Georgetown University in June 1942.
The Philippines had fallen. The Pacific fleet was still in
shambles at Pearl Harbor. German tanks smashed their

Al Blozis, collegiate record holder in the shot put: the Olympic dream unfulfilled. (Georgetown University)

way through Russia, heading to Stalingrad. And America was mobilizing for the monumental task ahead: the defeat of Japan and Nazi Germany.

Al Blozis had hoped to win a gold medal in the 1940 Summer Olympics in the shot put. Blozis, who stood six-foot-six and weighed 250 pounds, had shattered every shot put record that ever existed for a collegian. But thanks to Hitler and Tojo there would be no Olympic Games in 1940. Al Blozis's disappointment was tempered by the fact that he also played football. He was a tackle in an era when a player played both ways, offense and defense, each game. Blozis joined the Giants for the 1942 season after trying to get into every branch of the military. His great patriotism came up against his only obstacle—his size. Al Blozis was rejected simply because he was too big.

Blozis played the game with the ferocity and drive that marked him as an All-League selection in just his first season. Although he was enjoying tremendous success in football, his quest to join the military never wavered, and finally he was inducted into the army at the end of the 1943 season.

During basic training Al Blozis set a record for throwing a hand grenade. Because of his size Blozis's uniforms had to be specially tailored. He completed Officers Training School in the fall of 1944. The war was getting that much closer for Al Blozis.

Giants coach Steve Owen couldn't believe his good fortune when Lieutenant Al Blozis showed up at the Polo Grounds during his leave after being commissioned. Blozis put on a practice uniform and would play in the next two games, against Brooklyn (Brooklyn had a football team then, called the Dodgers) and the Washington Redskins.

Lieutenant Al Blozis played in the 1944 championship for the Giants against the Green Bay Packers, a game the Giants would lose, 14–7. Shortly thereafter, Al Blozis shipped overseas.

Six weeks after Blozis played in that championship game against Green Bay he went out in a snowstorm in the Vosges Mountains in France to search for a missing patrol and never returned. Al Blozis was listed as missing in action. A number of weeks later the army officially listed him as killed in action. Al Blozis was 26 years old. The Giants retired his jersey. No Giants player will ever wear number 32 again.

The Iron Man of Pro Football

Mel Hein. (New York Giants)

In an era before stadiums, end zone celebrations, salary caps, and league television contracts that could support several small-size nations, pro football players toiled on both sides of the ball. Perhaps no player was more proficient than Mel Hein, a charter member of the NFL Hall of Fame and the center and linebacker for the Giants from 1931 to 1945.

Hein stood six-foot-three and weighed 230 pounds. When he graduated from Washington State University the NFL draft was still several years away, so Hein wrote to the Giants asking for a tryout. The Giants wisely offered the Washington State All-American a contract, and the Iron Man's career began.

Mel Hein made All-League eight times and played in seven championship games. On offense he was a pulverizing blocker. As a linebacker, Hein was a deadly tackler and an alert pass defender. While playing for Washington State he once intercepted eight passes—in a single game. After Hein hung up the cleats, he coached in the old All-American Football Conference as well as at the University of Southern California. Hein would later become a supervisor of officials in the American Football Conference.

Mel Hein and Phil Simms share the Giants record for most seasons played with 15, but no Giant has ever played in as many games as Hein did—172. The only time in his career he came out of a game was when he broke his nose in a game against the Brooklyn Dodgers on Pearl Harbor day, 1941. That, however, proved to be just a minor pit stop, as he would later return to action in that game.

Mel Hein died on February 29, 1992, in San Clemente, California. It is fair to say that in the history of the NFL, no man played in as many minutes of game action as Mel Hein did during his career—or ever will.

THE EARLY YEARS: 1925–55

Answers:

1. 1925.

2. d. The Providence Steam Roller.

3. The exact amount is not known, but accounts vary that the sum was between $500 and $2,500.

4. Mara was a bookmaker, which in 1925 was legal.

5. Tom Folwell.

6. Jim Thorpe.

7. Red Grange.

8. b. 1933—the Giants and the Chicago Bears met in the first NFL championship game played in Chicago. The Giants lost, 23–21.

9. The 1934 NFL championship game, when the Giants donned sneakers at halftime to best the Chicago Bears, 30–13, on the icy Polo Grounds turf.

10. a. 7—the Giants appeared in the NFL title game in 1933, 1934, 1935, 1938, 1939, 1941, and 1944.

11. Mel Hein.

12. Cal Hubbard. Hubbard was one of the great linemen in the 1920s and 1930s and later pursued a career as a major league umpire.

13. d. 2—the Giants beat the Chicago Bears in 1934 and the Detroit Lions in 1938.

14. Al Blozis.

15. c. Jack Lummus—Lummus, an end from Baylor, was awarded the Congressional Medal of Honor posthumously after serving with the Marines on Iwo Jima in 1945.

16. b. Jim Lee Howell.

17. c. Sid Luckman.

18. Steve Owen.

19. c. Alphonse "Tuffy" Leemans.

20. b. Ward Cuff.

21. Art Lewis, a tackle from Ohio University, played just one season with the Giants.

22. Ken Strong.

23. a. The Brooklyn Dodgers.

24. c. Steve Owen—the legendary head coach finished with 151 wins.

25. Emlen Tunnell, a defensive back from Iowa, would eventually be elected to the NFL Hall of Fame.

26. Quarterback Frank Filchock and fullback Merle Hapes. Both players declined the bribe, and Filchock turned in a gritty performance in the loss to the Bears. Filchock and Hapes opted to play in Canada following this incident but were later reinstated, (Filchock in 1954, Hapes in 1954), allowing them to finish their careers in the NFL.

27. True.

28. Charlie Conerly.

29. Vince Lombardi.

30. Conerly—Mississippi; Price—Tulane; Landry—Texas; Grier—Penn State; DeRogatis—Duke.

31. b. Bill Swiacki.

32. 1952.

33. Hap Moran, who took off for a 91-yard gallop against the Green Bay Packers in 1930.

34. a. Gene "Choo-Choo" Roberts.

35. Ben Agajanian.

36. a. The Los Angeles Rams.

37. Otto Schnellbacher.

38. Ben Agajanian.

39. Arnie Weinmeister.

40. b. Tom Landry.

41. Jim Lee Howell.

42. Alex Webster.

43. Roosevelt Grier.

44. Roosevelt Brown.

45. d. Kyle Rote.

2

THE GLORY YEARS: 1956–63

Questions:

1. Who was quarterback Charlie Conerly's backup from 1954 to 1959? a. Bobby Clatterbuck b. Don Heinrich c. Tom Dublinski d. George Shaw

2. Which Giants defender is held to have said, "We try to hurt everybody. We hit each other as hard as we can. This is a man's game"? a. Harland Svare b. Rosey Grier c. Sam Huff d. Andy Robustelli

3. How many touchdown passes did quarterback Y. A. Tittle throw in 1963? a. 29 b. 27 c. 41 d. 36

4. Who centered the Giants offensive line in the 1950s and early 1960s?

5. Which Baltimore Colt scored the winning touchdown in sudden death overtime in the 1958 NFL championship game against the Giants?

6. Who was the former Brooklyn College quarterback who later served as head coach of the Giants?

7. Which Giants kicker booted a 49-yard field goal in a snowstorm against the Cleveland Browns in 1958 to put the Giants in a playoff game against those same Browns for the Eastern Conference crown?

8. True or False: Quarterback Charlie Conerly never led the NFL in passing.

9. Who was known as the Chief? a. Phil King b. Don Chandler c. Frank Gifford d. Sam Huff

10. Name the two members of the Giants defense who attended tiny Arnold College in Connecticut.

Sam Huff (70) and Chuck Bednarik (60), two Hall of Famers, square off in a Giants-Eagles tussle. (Dan Rubin)

11. Name the Eagles linebacker who knocked out Frank Gifford in a 1960 game, which led to Gifford retiring for one season.

12. Who scored the Giants' lone touchdown in the 1959 championship game rematch with the Baltimore Colts? a. Mel Triplett b. Bob Schnelker c. Phil King d. Joe Biscaha

13. Which Giants linebacker was the nemesis of the great Cleveland Browns running back Jim Brown?

14. Who did the Giants trade to the San Francisco 49ers in order to obtain quarterback Y. A. Tittle? a. Frank Youso b. Bob Simms c. Lou Cordileone d. Ed Sutton

15. Name the Brooklyn native and 1936 Olympic sprint hopeful who served as the radio voice of the Giants.

16. Who was known as Little Mo?

17. Name the rookie halfback who began his 14-year Giants career in 1959.

18. Name the Giants defensive back who scored three touchdowns on interception returns in 1963.

19. Who was Y. A. Tittle's favorite target from 1961 through 1963? a. Del Shofner b. Joe Walton c. Frank Gifford d. Paul Dudley

20. What was Y. A. Tittle's jersey number, which has been retired?

21. Who was the Giants kicker who handled both the punting and placekicking from 1962 through 1964?

22. What was the score of the 1958 sudden death overtime championship game between the Giants and the Baltimore Colts? a. 23–16 b. 24–17 c. 26–20 d. 23–17

23. What was the score of the 1959 Giants–Baltimore Colts NFL championship game? a. 40–17 b. 35–12 c. 31–16 d. 24–13

24. Match the player with his alma mater:

Sam Huff	LSU
Del Shofner	Notre Dame
Dick Lynch	Baylor
Joe Walton	West Virginia
Y. A. Tittle	Pittsburgh

25. Name the clubhouse man who designed the play that worked for a touchdown in the crucial game against the Eagles in 1961.

26. What was the nature of Y. A. Tittle's injury in the 1963 NFL championship game? a. Groin pull b. Sprained knee c. Concussion d. Separated shoulder

27. Which Eastern Division foe did the Giants humiliate 53–0 in a 1961 game at Yankee Stadium? a. The Los Angeles Rams b. The Detroit Lions c. The San Francisco 49ers d. The Washington Redskins

28. Who was the sure-handed, undersized tight end of the Y. A. Tittle years? a. Joe Walton b. Del Shofner c. Lee Grosscup d. Allan Webb

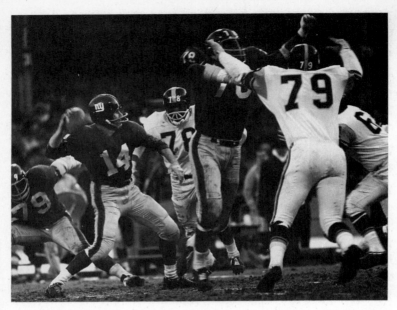

Y. A. Tittle (14) in action against the Pittsburgh Steelers. (Dan Rubin)

29. Who was the halfback who wore number 13 for the Giants and wore the same number as a New York Titans and New York Jets receiver?

30. Name the University of Utah quarterback who was a first-round draft pick in 1959 but had a short career in the NFL.

31. Which Giants defensive back went 102 yards for a touchdown with an interception return against the Dallas Cowboys in a 1961 game? a. Carl "Spider" Lockhart b. Erich Barnes c. Dick Nolan d. Jimmy Patton

32. Name the Giant who scored the lone touchdown for the team in the championship title game losses to the Green Bay Packers in both 1961 and 1962. a. Sam Horner b. Johnny Counts c. Jim Collier d. Alex Webster

33. Who was the rookie quarterback who replaced Y. A. Tittle after Tittle went down with an injury in the 1963 title game against the Chicago Bears?

34. Who was the first Giant to gain more than 1,000 yards on pass receptions? a. Del Shofner b. Homer Jones c. Frank Gifford d. Kyle Rote

35. Name the quarterback who replaced the oft-injured Charlie Conerly during the 1960 season.

36. Which Eastern Conference foe introduced the safety blitz to upset the Giants in the 1961 season opener, 21–10? a. The Dallas Cowboys b. The St. Louis Cardinals c. The Cleveland Browns d. The Washington Redskins

37. How many times did Y. A. Tittle throw seven touchdown passes in a game, tying an NFL record? a. Three times b. Two times c. Five times d. Once

38. Which Giants running back had a big comeback year in 1961, leading the team in rushing? a. Frank Gifford b. Alex Webster c. Joel Wells d. Bob Gaiters

39. What was the final score of the 1961 championship game against the Green Bay Packers?

40. In which round was Joe Morrison drafted in the 1959 NFL draft?

41. Which Giant appeared on the cover of *Time* magazine in November 1959? a. Sam Huff b. Frank Gifford c. Charley Conerly d. Rosey Grier

42. Name the former San Francisco 49er and Hall of Fame running back the Giants picked up prior to the start of the 1963 season.

43. Which Brooklyn high school did Giants head coach Allie Sherman attend? a. Brooklyn Tech b. Boys High School c. Canarsie High School d. Erasmus Hall High School

44. Which team did the Giants play the weekend of President Kennedy's assassination? a. The Baltimore Colts b. The Dallas Cowboys c. The St. Louis Cardinals d. The Washington Redskins

45. How many 300-yard passing games did Y. A. Tittle have during the 1962 season? a. 4 b. 6 c. 7 d. 1

Giants defense in action in 1961 game against the Cardinals. (Dan Rubin)

46. Name the Giants linebacker from the late 1950s who later became an NFL head coach.

47. Who is the Giants all-time leading pass receiver, with 395 catches? a. Del Shofner b. Kyle Rote c. Joe Morrison d. Frank Gifford

48. How many championship games did Frank Gifford play in? a. 7 b. 3 c. 6 d. 5

49. Match the player with his alma mater:

Dick Modzelewski	Purdue
Jack Stroud	UCLA
Bill Stits	Tennessee
Phil King	Maryland
Erich Barnes	Vanderbilt

50. Who was defensive tackle Rosey Grier traded to the Los Angeles Rams for in 1963? a. Jim Moran b. John Lovetere c. Stan Fanning d. Lamar Lundy

51. Which year did the Giants move from the Polo Grounds to Yankee Stadium? a. 1957 b. 1956 c. 1961 d. 1959

52. Which year was Frank Gifford voted the NFL Player of the Year? a. 1958 b. 1960 c. 1959 d. 1956

53. Which team did the Giants beat for the 1956 NFL title? a. The Chicago Bears b. The Chicago Cardinals c. The Cleveland Browns d. The San Francisco 49ers

54. Name the two Giants running backs who scored touchdowns in the 1956 championship game against the Chicago Bears.

55. What was Frank Gifford's jersey number?

The Giant with a Heart

Emlen Tunnell. (New York Giants)

It was 1948, the year after Jackie Robinson first stepped up to the plate at Ebbets Field in Brooklyn, breaking the color barrier in major league baseball, when Emlen Tunnell walked into the Giants offices and asked for a tryout. Emlen Tunnell was granted his tryout—and lucky for the Giants, who found themselves a star. Emlen Tunnell found himself on an NFL roster and in doing so became the first African American to play for the New York Giants.

Tunnell played for the Giants from 1948 through 1958 in head coach Steve Owen's Umbrella Defense. He played alongside such stars as Otto Schnellbacher, Harmon Rowe, and Tom Landry in the Giants secondary and holds the team record for career interceptions with 74, as well as many team punt-return records.

At the time of Emlen Tunnell's death at the still young age of 50 he was the Giants assistant director of player personnel. He also served as a scout and assistant coach. Despite his exploits on the field he was best remembered by his teammates as a caring and compassionate man.

"He was good to all people. He was a hell of a decent person," teammate Andy Robustelli said of Tunnell. No story, though, illustrates this better than the "day" the Giants celebrated for Tunnell in his final season with them in 1958. On his way to the stadium, Tunnell was stopped by a number of men standing outside the entrance to Yankee Stadium who gave him what he would consider the most touching gift he would receive that day. They were homeless men who had passed the hat around for their friend who had never forgotten them. They raised $28.

"It was the best gift," he later explained, "because if they had a million bucks, they'd have given it to me. They were guys who hung around the ballpark, guys I'd given a dime or quarter to when I started playing at the Polo Grounds, and then they hung around Yankee Stadium when the Giants moved there."

Emlen Tunnell capped his illustrious career in the pros by being the first African American to be named an assistant coach in the NFL. He was the Giants defensive backfield coach in the mid-1960s. In 1967 he achieved another first—the first African American inducted into the pro football Hall of Fame.

Big Rosey

During his 12-year NFL career, spanning the years from 1955 to 1967, Roosevelt Grier was considered one of the most formidable defensive tackles in the league. The six-foot-five-inch, 300-pound Grier played on five Eastern Conference championship teams as well as on the 1956 Giants team that beat the Chicago Bears, 47–7, to win the NFL title. He was named to the All-Pro team that season.

In 1963, Roosevelt Grier was traded to the Los Angeles Rams for defensive tackle John Lovetere, and for the next five seasons Grier became a vital cog in the Rams' Fearsome Foursome defensive line that featured Hall of Famers David "Deacon" Jones, Merlin Olsen, and Lamar Lundy.

Though bitter and angry at his trade to the Rams, Grier settled into the L.A. scene and began to pursue his other passions, music and acting. He appeared and sang on many television variety shows and recorded a couple of songs. Grier also acted on several television series, including *The Man from U.N.C.L.E., Daniel Boone,* and *Mr. Novak,* but Grier soon proved to be a man of other callings.

Among teammates Grier was known for his kindness and compassion. He admitted that one of his biggest fears as a player was that he could injure an opponent. In the years following his retirement from the game, Grier has tried to make the world a better place through his many acts of kindness. He has been a political activist, best remembered as Robert F. Kennedy's bodyguard that tragic night in Los Angeles in 1968 when Kennedy was assassinated by Sirhan Sirhan. It was Grier who wrestled the pistol away from Sirhan after the fatal shots were fired. "He killed my dream," Grier recently said in an interview when asked about that sorrowful night.

This gentle giant has been a devotee of needlepoint. "I get keyed up a lot, you know, and I can sit and do something like this and kind of get away from it all," he once said about his hobby. Grier even published a book in 1973 about his relaxing passion, *Rosey Grier's Needlepoint for Men.*

Roosevelt Grier is now a minister. He has worked for the Special Olympics and has headed literacy programs in Los Angeles. Roosevelt Grier has also visited O. J. Simpson in the Los Angeles County Jail. Wherever Grier has gone he continues to preach his gospel of compassion, brotherhood, and love.

Plugged-in Giants

Paul Brown was considered one of the most innovative coaches in the history of the NFL. Brown was responsible for such breakthroughs as the playbook, the face mask, and the draw play, and he was the first head coach to place his assistant coaches in the press box complete with phones to contact the sidelines during the game. In 1956, Paul Brown might have even outdone himself when he decided to put a radio receiver in his quarterback's helmet. During the course of the game Brown would transmit plays to his quarterback through a hand mike.

The Giants began the 1956 season on the road at Cleveland. They were prepared for the Browns' electronic gadgetry. Bob Topp, a former Michigan end who was on the Giants payroll, operated a radio receiver on the Giants bench and picked up Paul Brown's instructions to his quarterback, George Ratterman. Gene Filipski, a halfback the Giants acquired from Cleveland several weeks earlier, was held in readiness in the event Brown went with a number system to call his plays.

Once the game started Topp relayed the Browns' instructions to Tom Landry, the Giants defensive coach, who would then shout the Cleveland offensive plays to his players on the field. Throughout the game the Giants stymied the Cleveland offense.

After the game Paul Brown complained that due to crowd noises he used the radio only on the first series of downs. The Giants' 21–9 victory that day was their first triumph over the Browns in three seasons. Several other teams also tried electronic devices to send plays into games, but by midseason NFL commissioner Bert Bell ordered a league-wide ban on all electronic gadgetry.

The Apprenticeship of
Vince and Tom

Before Vince Lombardi went to Green Bay and became an NFL icon and before Tom Landry headed down to Dallas to become the fabled "man in the hat," they learned the pro coaching trade as assistant coaches in the 1950s with the Giants under Jim Lee Howell.

Vince Lombardi was recruited from the Army coaching staff, where he served under the legendary Army head coach Earl "Red" Blaik as the backfield coach. He left West Point in 1954 to become the Giants offensive coach. "Vince Lombardi," Frank Gifford has said, "is responsible for my success." Prior to Lombardi's arrival with the Giants, Gifford had played cornerback and safety as well as seeing spot duty on offense. Lombardi told Gifford on the first day of training camp in 1954 that he was his halfback. Gifford later admitted that Lombardi's faith in him was a confidence builder. During his tenure as the Giants offensive coach from 1954 through 1958, Vince Lombardi revamped and ran the offense for Jim Lee Howell.

Though he was one of Fordham University's famed Seven Blocks of Granite in the 1930s and a classmate of Giants owner Wellington Mara, Lombardi never played professional football. Instead, while he was with the Giants, Vince Lombardi learned the pro game and sharpened his coaching techniques. What Lombardi learned while with the Giants proved invaluable at Green Bay, as Lombardi was laying the foundation for the Packers dynasty of the 1960s, when Green Bay would go on to win five league titles.

While Vince Lombardi ran the offense, Tom Landry ran the defense. The former University of Texas quarterback was picked up from the old All-American Football Conference in 1950 and served the Giants well as both a defensive back and defensive coach before he left to become the first head coach for the Dallas Cowboys, in 1960. Teammate Frank Gifford said Landry

Head-to-head collision: The Tom Landry–coached defense in action in 1959 battle with the Browns as Sam Huff (70) sticks it to Jim Brown. (Dan Rubin)

had a knack of knowing what plays the offense would call. In 1954, Landry assumed the dual role of player and defensive coach.

Landry wore those two hats during the 1954 and 1955 seasons, and in 1955, after his final season as a player, he became solely the team's defensive coach. Landry is credited as having been the innovator of the 4–3 defense, and in an era before computers and video, he broke down the opponents' films and studied their offense, looking for tendencies. During Landry's coaching tenure from 1954 through 1959, the Giants played in three NFL championship games.

Though he once admitted that he never had any ambition to be a head coach, Tom Landry left the Giants in 1960 to lead the Dallas Cowboys in their maiden season in the NFL. Tom Landry put together a string of 20 consecutive winning seasons and two Super Bowl triumphs during his 29 years as head coach of the Cowboys. It is fair to say Tom Landry and Vince Lombardi gained invaluable experience during coaching apprenticeships with the Giants long before their great head-coaching talents were exposed.

"The Best Football Game Ever Played"

After beating the Cleveland Browns in a 1958 conference playoff game, 10–0, the Giants won the right to fight it out with the Baltimore Colts for the NFL championship on December 28 at Yankee Stadium.

The 1958 Colts would place five of its members in the Hall of Fame: quarterback Johnny Unitas, halfback Lenny Moore, wide receiver Raymond Berry, offensive tackle Jim Parker, and defensive end Gino Marchetti. They had a record identical to the Giants' for the season: nine wins and three losses.

Sixty-four thousand fans huddled into Yankee Stadium on that cold December afternoon. Due to television contracts with the NFL at the time, the game was blacked out in the New York area. At the same time a newspaper strike crippled news-starved New Yorkers, thus making it impossible for them to read about the game.

The Giants drew first blood as Pat Summerall accounted for all the first-quarter scoring himself, nailing a 36-yard field goal. The second quarter, though, belonged to the Colts, who threatened to blow the Giants out of Yankee Stadium. Their fullback, Alan Ameche, carried the ball in from two yards out for the first Colts touchdown, and later that period Johnny Unitas hit Raymond Berry in the end zone with a 15-yard strike, giving Baltimore a 14–3 halftime lead.

A goal-line stand sparked the Giants in the third quarter. New York moved the ball smartly downfield, the key play on the drive being a long pass from quarterback Charlie Conerly to Kyle Rote, who hauled it in and took it down to the Colts 25-yard line. Only one glitch on the play: Rote left the ball on the ground. Luckily, Johnny-on-the-spot teammate Alex Webster recovered the fumble and headed for the Colts end zone before being tackled on the one-yard line. Mel Triplett took it in on

Alan Ameche ends "The Best Football Game Ever Played" as he crosses the goal line in sudden-death overtime in the 1958 NFL championship game. (AP/Wide World Photos)

the next play, and the Giants were back in the game, having cut the Colts lead to 14–10.

In the fourth quarter, with the Colts still clinging to their four-point lead, the Giants struck again. Conerly hit Frank Gifford with a 15-yard touchdown pass, and suddenly the Giants had their first lead since the first quarter, 17–14. Visions of an NFL title floated through the minds of the Giants faithful. However, a legend—and history—was about to be made.

With two minutes to go in the game, the Colts took possession of the ball on their own 14-yard line. Johnny Unitas coolly picked apart the Giants defense, moving Baltimore downfield to the Giants 13-yard line with seven seconds to play. Steve Myra was called on by Baltimore coach Weeb Ewbank to tie the game. When he booted a 27-yard field goal, evening the score at 17–all, he forced the first-ever sudden death overtime game in NFL championship game history.

In the overtime the Giants took the ball first but were

halted by the Colts defense. Following a Don Chandler punt, Baltimore took over the ball on their own 20-yard line. Once again Johnny Unitas coolly led his team down the field. The drive, and the game, culminated as Alan Ameche bulled across the goal line from the two-yard line, giving Baltimore the NFL championship, 23–17.

Millions of fans across America watched the sudden death game. The Giants-Colts battle caught the imagination of the nation, and the television industry realized that it had a gem in covering pro football. In the January 5, 1959, issue of *Sports Illustrated,* writer Tex Maule, who covered the game, headlined his piece, THE BEST FOOTBALL GAME EVER PLAYED.

Close but No Cigar

From 1958 through 1963 the Giants appeared in five NFL championship games, but the football gods didn't smile on the boys from the Big Apple. The sad stories are as follows.

1958: The Baltimore Colts beat the Giants in sudden death overtime, 23–17, at Yankee Stadium, the game just described.

1959: In a rematch of their 1958 overtime classic, this time in Baltimore, the Giants took a 9–7 lead into the fourth quarter, but the Colts exploded for 24 points as Johnny Unitas ran for a touchdown, threw for another, and Johnny Sample picked off a Charlie Conerly pass and ran it back for yet another Colts score as Baltimore beat the Giants, 31–16.

1961: The Giants traveled to frigid Green Bay, Wisconsin, to take on Vince Lombardi's Packers. The Packers and the arctic conditions hampered the Giants passing attack as Y. A. Tittle and Charlie Conerly threw for only 119 yards between them, and the Giants suffered their most humiliating defeat in a title game, 37–0.

1962: The Giants sought revenge for their embarrassing 1961 title game loss to Green Bay in the rematch against Vince Lombardi's powerful 13–1 Packers at Yankee Stadium. Again the Giants were facing arctic conditions—and they weren't even in Green Bay this time—as 40-mile-per-hour winds and a wind chill factor of nearly zero virtually nullified Y. A. Tittle's pass-oriented offense. The game turned into a brutal smashmouth contest in which Green Bay fullback Jim Taylor and Giants middle linebacker Sam Huff fought a violent battle with one another throughout the game. At one point Taylor, following a vicious Huff hit, swallowed his tongue. At the final gun, however, the Giants were bested again, 16–7.

1963: During the regular season Y. A. Tittle threw for a Giants season record 36 touchdown passes, and the G-men placed eight players on the Pro Bowl team,

1962 NFL championship game at Yankee Stadium: Giants vs. Packers. (Dan Rubin)

finishing 11–3. They squared off against the Chicago Bears in the championship game December 29 at Wrigley Field in Chicago.

The Giants once again faced weather conditions that hampered their pass-oriented offense with high winds, nine-degree temperatures, and a knee injury to Tittle. The Bears held on for a 14–10 win and the NFL championship.

The bitter loss to the Bears that day ended the Giants' Glory Years, as the team would begin an 18-year descent into NFL wasteland, wandering about the NFL desert until 1981, when they would reward their devoutly loyal fans with a playoff berth.

THE GLORY YEARS: 1956–63

Answers:

1. b. Don Heinrich.

2. c. Sam Huff.

3. d. 36—still a Giants single-season record for most touchdown passes.

4. Ray Wietecha.

5. Alan Ameche.

6. Allie Sherman.

7. Pat Summerall.

8. False—Charlie Conerly led the NFL in passing in 1959.

9. a. Phil King.

10. Andy Robustelli and Alan Webb.

11. Chuck Bednarik.

12. b. Bob Schnelker.

13. Sam Huff.

14. c. Guard Lou Cordileone.

15. Marty Glickman.

16. Defensive tackle Dick Modzelewski.

17. Joe Morrison.

18. Dick Lynch.

19. a. Del Shofner.

20. #14.

21. Don Chandler.

22. d. The Colts won 23–17.

23. c. The Colts won again, 31–16.

24. Huff—West Virginia; Shofner—Baylor; Lynch—Notre Dame; Walton—Pittsburgh; Tittle—LSU.

25. Pete Previte.

26. b. Tittle suffered a sprained knee.

27. d. The Washington Redskins.

28. a. Joe Walton.

29. Don Maynard.

30. Lee Grosscup.

31. b. Erich Barnes.

32. c. Jim Collier.

33. Glynn Griffing.

34. a. Del Shofner.

35. George Shaw.

36. b. The St. Louis Cardinals.

37. d. Only once.

38. b. Alex Webster.

39. Green Bay won 37–0.

40. The third.

41. a. Sam Huff.

42. Hugh McElhenny.

43. b. Boys High School.

44. c. The St. Louis Cardinals.

45. a. Four.

46. Harland Svare.

47. c. Joe Morrison, with 395 receptions.

48. d. Five.

49. Modzelewski—Maryland; Stroud—Tennessee; Stits—UCLA; King—Vanderbilt; Barnes—Purdue.

50. b. John Lovetere.

51. b. 1956.

52. d. 1956.

53. a. The Chicago Bears.

54. Mel Triplett and Alex Webster.

55. #16.

3

WANDERING IN THE GRIDIRON DESERT: 1964–80

Questions:

1. The Giants recorded their worst record when they finished 1–12–1. What season did that take place? a. 1983 b. 1973 c. 1966 d. 1980

2. Which team was Sam Huff traded to? a. The Detroit Lions b. The Washington Redskins c. The Chicago Bears d. The Pittsburgh Steelers

3. Name the Cornell University quarterback who spelled Y. A. Tittle in Tittle's final season.

4. What year did both Frank Gifford and Alex Webster retire? a. 1964 b. 1965 c. 1963 d. 1967

5. True or False: Tucker Frederickson was the NFL rookie of the year in 1965.

6. Name the tackle from the University of Missouri taken by the Giants in the first round of the 1966 draft.

7. Who was the quarterback who helped guide the Giants to a 7–7 record in 1965 and would later share quarterback duties with Bob Griese during the Miami Dolphins' perfect 17–0 season in 1972? a. Earl Morrall b. Norm Snead c. George Mira d. Milt Plum

8. Who was the first Giants running back to rush for more than 1,000 yards in a season? a. Joe Morris b. Frank Gifford c. Joe Morrison d. Ron Johnson

9. Who won, and what was the final score, of the first Giants-Jets regular season game? a. Giants, 31–13 b. Jets, 21–20 c. Giants, 17–10 d. Giants, 22–10

Tucker Frederickson. (New York Giants)

10. Name the Hungarian soccer-style kicker the Giants picked up from the Buffalo Bills in 1964.

11. Name the gritty tackle from Grambling University who played in the middle of the Giants defensive line in the 1970s.

12. The Giants traded quarterback Fran Tarkenton back to the Minnesota Vikings for which veteran quarterback? a. John Hadl b. Jack Concannon c. Norm Snead d. Frank Ryan

13. Name the sure-handed receiver who was also acquired by the Giants from Minnesota in the Fran Tarkenton deal.

14. The NFL record for total points in a single game was set in the Giants' 72–41 loss to which team? a. The Philadelphia Eagles b. The Washington Redskins c. The Baltimore Colts d. The Cleveland Browns

15. Name the bizarre-acting running back the Giants took in the first round of the NFL draft and later traded to the Baltimore Colts in 1964.

16. Which former Giants star became head football coach at the University of South Carolina?

17. Who was the speedster from Texas Southern University who holds the record for the longest Giants touchdown reception? a. Coleman Zeno b. Rocky Thompson c. Earnest Gray d. Homer Jones

18. Which season was the first for the Giants to call the Meadowlands home? a. 1976 b. 1977 c. 1975 d. 1974

19. What was the final score of the first game played by the Giants at Giants Stadium in the Meadowlands?

20. Who scored the first touchdown by the Giants at the Meadlowlands? a. Jimmy Robinson b. Doug Kotar c. Craig Morton d. Larry Csonka

21. How many seasons did Fran Tarkenton play for the Giants? a. 3 b. 5 c. 6 d. 4

22. Who replaced Allie Sherman as Giants coach in 1969?

23. Name the wiry, skillful safety who played with the Giants from 1965 to 1975 and had 41 career interceptions.

24. How many 1,000-yard-rushing seasons did Ron Johnson have?

25. Who was the Philadelphia Eagles defender who scored a touchdown after the fumbled handoff between Joe Pisarcik and Larry Csonka in the infamous 1978 game at the Meadowlands?

Alex Webster served the Giants as player and coach. (New York Giants)

26. What year was linebacker Harry Carson drafted?

27. Which team was Homer Jones traded to in 1970? a. The New Orleans Saints b. The Atlanta Falcons c. The Cleveland Browns˙d. The Buffalo Bills

28. The Giants, and Giants fans, were expecting big things from the 1973 Giants team that went 6–0 in the preseason but were sadly disappointed once the regular season began. What was the Giants' record during the regular season that year?

29. Who coached the Giants from 1976 to 1978?

30. Who was the solid defensive tackle and first-round draft pick from Colorado who was killed in an auto accident in 1979?

31. Which Giant led the NFC in receiving in 1971? a. Bob Tucker b. Rich Houston c. Dick Kotite d. Junior Coffey

32. How many seasons did Larry Csonka play for the Giants?

33. What former Giant quarterbacked the Denver Broncos to a surprising appearance in Super Bowl XII?

34. What was the NFC-leading number of passes caught in 1971? a. 61 b. 59 c. 70 d. 64

35. Who was the Michigan State University safety who chose professional football over baseball and had an outstanding career as a Giants linebacker from 1973 to 1983?

36. Match the player with his alma mater:

Ron Johnson	North Texas State
Bob Tucker	Cal Lutheran
Carl Lockhart	South Carolina State
Harry Carson	Bloomsburg State
Brian Kelley	Michigan

37. Who did Joe Pisarcik play for before joining the Giants? a. The Philadelphia Eagles b. The New York Stars (World Football League) c. The Calgary Stampeders d. The Bridgeport Jets (East Coast Football League)

38. Who did the Giants play and what was the final score of the Giants' last game at Yankee Stadium on September 23, 1973? a. Dallas 27, Giants 21 b. Giants 14, St. Louis 7 c. Giants 16, Baltimore 13 d. Giants 23, Philadelphia 23

39. Name the team the Giants had to beat in the final game of the 1970 season to qualify for the playoffs and the final score.

40. Name the Ohio State University Buckeye who as a rookie in 1964 was drafted by both the Giants and the Jets and which team he chose to play with.

41. Name the free-spirited Giants defensive end from San Diego State University who has been a leading man on television and in film.

42. Who was the slashing Giants running back from the University of Kentucky who led the team in rushing in 1976 and 1978 and died of cancer in 1983?

43. Who was the solid veteran pass-rushing defensive end the Giants picked up from the Cleveland Browns before the 1972 season? a. Charlie Harper b. Dan Goich c. Jack Gregory d. Pat Hughes

44. Who was the tight end for the Giants in the late 1960s and early 1970s who has served as an NFL head coach? a. Tom Gatewood b. Rich Kotite c. Bob Tucker d. Bob Crespino

45. Giants draftniks booed the team's first-round draft pick in 1979, a quarterback who led a small college to a 2–6–1 record the year before. Who was that pick?

46. Which year did George Young become the Giants general manager? a. 1980 b. 1977 c. 1981 d. 1979

47. True or False: Before the Giants beat the Redskins 12–9 in a 1976 game at Giants Stadium, the Redskins had a 12-game winning streak against New York.

48. What job did Ray Perkins hold before he was named as Giants head coach in 1979?

49. How many touchdown passes did Phil Simms throw in his rookie season of 1979? a. 13 b. 16 c. 14 d. 9

50. Who led the Giants in receiving in 1979—most of the passes being thrown by fellow Morehead State alumnus Phil Simms?

51. True or False: The Giants shut down O. J. Simpson on a Monday night game in 1975.

Carl "Spider" Lockhart, a tough, smart safety during the Giants' lean years. (New York Giants)

52. Which team did George Young come over from to be Giants general manager? a. The San Diego Chargers b. The Tampa Bay Buccaneers c. The Miami Dolphins d. The Oakland Raiders

53. Name the Giants player credited with inventing the spike.

54. Which pro football team did Ray Perkins play for? a. The Kansas City Chiefs b. The Baltimore Colts c. The Denver Broncos d. The Boston Patriots

55. Name the Giants wide receiver who caught four touchdown passes in a 1980 game against the St. Louis Cardinals.

56. When the Giants moved into Giants Stadium in 1976, that became their fifth home stadium. Name the other four.

57. Which Giants running back led the team in rushing in 1979 and is now a sportscaster? a. Billy Taylor b. Emery Moorehead c. Bobby Hammond d. Bo Matthews

The Saga of
Joe Don Looney

Even though Joe Don Looney was tossed off the University of Oklahoma football team three games into his senior season for fighting with an assistant coach, the Giants made him their number one pick in the NFL draft for the 1964 season.

The Giants were intrigued by the former Sooners running back's size and speed. Looney packed 230 rock-solid pounds on a six-foot-two-inch frame and could run the hundred-yard dash in 9.5 seconds. Difficulties, though, soon arose when Joe Don reported to the Giants training camp at Fairfield, Connecticut, in the summer of 1964.

Refusing to speak to reporters, Looney told them he was in training camp to play football, not to talk, and though he displayed unusual speed for a man his size, there were other problems in dealing with Joe Don. Looney refused to attend team meetings, skipped a number of practices, and was fined numerous times for refusing to have his ankles taped. He also balked at having the team trainer look at his leg after he pulled a muscle, telling head coach Allie Sherman, "It's my leg, not the trainer's." Y. A. Tittle reached out to Looney and asked him if he would like to attend a pregame meeting before an exhibition game. Looney declined, saying, "I don't know, Y. A., I gotta rest up." After 28 days in training camp, the Giants traded Looney to the Baltimore Colts.

Joe Don Looney bounced from Baltimore to Washington to Detroit to New Orleans, with an army stint in Vietnam thrown in along the way. He maintained his noncomformist ways and never stayed with any of those clubs for too long.

Certainly, Joe Don Looney never lived up to the enormous football greatness many had predicted for him. Rather, years of drug addiction and, later, enchantment with Eastern religion dominated Looney's life. He fol-

Enigmatic Joe Don Looney: a haunting legacy of unfulfilled potential. (University of Oklahoma)

lowed his guru, Swami Baba Muktananda, to India, where he tended his guru's elephant.

After time, though, Looney grew disenchanted with Baba Muktananda and returned to the United States, settling in his native Texas. Joe Don Looney was killed in a motorcycle accident near his Texas home in 1988. He was 45 years old.

The First Spiker

Homer Jones, en route to the end zone—and a spike! (Dan Rubin)

Homer Jones played flanker for the Giants from 1964 through 1969. He was a sturdily built man who sometimes ran pass patterns that weren't in the playbook. Quarterback Earl Morrall once said that Jones was so fast he could outrun a 70-yard pass.

Homer Jones finished his NFL career with the Cleveland Browns in 1970, but Jones is best remembered as a Giant. He is in the Giants record book for most touchdown passes caught in a season: 13 in 1967; longest reception for a touchdown: 98 yards against the Steelers in 1966; highest average per catch for a season: 24.7 yards in 1967; highest average per catch for a career: 22.6 yards on 214 career receptions; and also most yards receiving in a season: 1,209 in 1967. But Homer

Jones is also remembered by some as the NFL's first spiker.

Homer Jones promised that when he scored his first touchdown in the NFL he would throw the ball up into the stands. However, he also remembered the league rule that there was a $500 fine for such a celebration.

Jones recalled that when he crossed the goal line in a crucial game in the mid-1960s, instead of throwing the ball into the stands and having the fine levied against him by the league, he threw the ball on the ground emphatically, and the spike was born.

WANDERING IN THE GRIDIRON DESERT: 1964–80

Answers:

1. c. 1966.

2. b. The Washington Redskins.

3. Gary Wood.

4. a. At the end of the 1964 season.

5. False—it was Gale Sayers of the Chicago Bears.

6. Francis Peay.

7. a. Earl Morrall.

8. d. Ron Johnson.

9. d. The Giants, 22–10, in a 1970 game at Shea Stadium.

10. Pete Gogolak.

11. John Mendenhall.

12. c. Norm Snead.

13. Bob Grim.

14. b. The Washington Redskins.

15. Joe Don Looney.

16. Joe Morrison.

17. d. Homer Jones had a 98-yard reception against the Pittsburgh Steelers in 1966.

18. a. 1976.

19. The Giants lost to the Dallas Cowboys 24–14 on October 10, 1976.

20. a. Jimmy Robinson on a pass from Craig Morton against the Dallas Cowboys.

21. b. Five, 1967–71.

22. Alex Webster.

23. Carl Lockhart.

24. Two.

25. Herman Edwards.

26. 1976.

27. c. The Cleveland Browns.

28. 2–11–1.

29. John McVay.

30. Troy Archer.

31. a. Bob Tucker.

32. Three seasons, 1976–78.

33. Craig Morton.

34. b. 59.

35. Brad Van Pelt.

36. Johnson—Michigan; Tucker—Bloomsburg State; Lockhart—North Texas State; Carson—South Carolina State; Kelley—Cal Lutheran.

37. c. The Calgary Stampeders of the Canadian Football League.

38. d. The Giants and Eagles tied at 23-all.

39. The Los Angeles Rams, who beat the Giants 31–3.

40. Matt Snell—the Jets.

41. Fred Dryer.

42. Doug Kotar.

43. c. Jack Gregory.

44. b. Rich Kotite.

45. Phil Simms.

46. d. 1979.

47. True.

48. Ray Perkins was the offensive coordinator for the San Diego Chargers.

49. a. 13.

50. Gary Shirk.

51. Simpson managed his yards in that game—128 yards rushing—but the Giants won the game over the previously undefeated Buffalo Bills.

52. George Young was director of player personnel for the Miami Dolphins.

53. Homer Jones.

54. b. Ray Perkins was a wide receiver for the Baltimore Colts from 1967 to 1971.

55. Earnest Gray.

56. The Polo Grounds, Yankee Stadium, the Yale Bowl, and Shea Stadium.

57. a. Billy Taylor.

4

REBIRTH AND TRIUMPH: 1981–90

Questions:

1. Who was the powerful running back the Giants picked up from the Houston Oilers during the 1981 season?

2. True or False: Bill Parcells was once an assistant coach at Navy.

3. Which season was Lawrence Taylor's rookie season?

4. Name the player selected ahead of Lawrence Taylor in the NFL draft.

Phil Simms leads the way for the Giants in their Super Bowl XXI win over Denver. (Jerry Pinkus)

5. Which Giants kicker made the overtime field goal in the final regular season game against the Dallas Cowboys to help put the Giants in the 1981 playoffs—their first playoff appearance in eighteen years? a. Ali Haji-Sheikh b. Joe Danelo c. Dave Jennings d. Eric Schubert

6. For which college team did Ray Perkins leave the Giants toward the end of the 1982 season to become head coach? a. Auburn b. Tennessee c. Purdue d. Alabama

7. Which Giants linebacker picked off a Danny White pass in sudden death overtime in the 1981 season finale against the Dallas Cowboys that helped set up the winning field goal? a. Brad Van Pelt b. Lawrence Taylor c. Byron Hunt d. Harry Carson

8. In 1981, when the Giants qualified for their first playoff game in 18 years, they played the Philadelphia Eagles in an NFC wild card game. What was the final score? a. Eagles 36, Giants 20 b. Giants 27, Eagles 21 c. Giants 17, Eagles 10 d. Giants 16, Eagles 13 in overtime

9. Which year did Phil Simms pass for a Giants team record 4,004 yards? a. 1986 b. 1985 c. 1989 d. 1984

10. Match the player with his alma mater:

Joe Morris	Oregon
Mark Bavaro	Michigan State
George Martin	Syracuse
Carl Banks	Iowa State
Karl Nelson	Notre Dame

11. Who said, "Once a Giant, always a Giant, that's loyalty that remains." a. Pat Summerall b. Frank Gifford c. Allie Sherman d. Fran Tarkenton

12. Who was the quarterback chosen by Bill Parcells as the Giants starting quarterback over Phil Simms in Parcells's first season as head coach?

13. What was linebacking great Harry Carson's jersey number?

14. Which Giant holds the record for most touchdowns scored by a defensive lineman?

15. Which team did Brad Van Pelt join after he left the Giants? a. The Houston Oilers b. The New England Patriots c. The Los Angeles Raiders d. The Los Angeles Rams

16. In a 1982 Thanksgiving Day game, Lawrence Taylor scored a 97-yard touchdown against which team?

17. Name the blocking back who cleared the way for Joe Morris.

18. Which season was the first in which Joe Morris gained 1,000 yards rushing? a. 1985 b. 1988 c. 1984 d. 1986

19. Who was the tight end for the Giants who scored their first touchdown in Super Bowl XXI against the Denver Broncos?

20. Who was the All-Pro cornerback from the University of Colorado traded by the Giants to the Denver Broncos in 1986?

Ed Mcaffrey

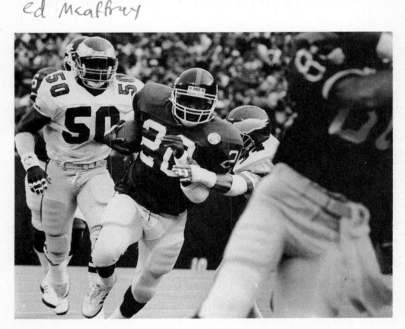

Joe Morris eludes Eagles defenders and heads upfield. (Jerry Pinkus)

21. Who was the Giants receiver who caught a crucial fourth-down-and-18-yards-to-go pass against the Minnesota Vikings in a key 1986 game leading to a Giants victory? a. Phil McConkey b. Stacy Robinson c. Lionel Manuel d. Bobby Johnson

22. Name the placekicker released by the Giants but then called back by the team for a 1985 game against the Tampa Bay Buccaneers—a game in which he kicked five field goals.

23. What is the Giants record for pass completions in a game? a. 37 by Phil Simms in 1989 b. 40 by Phil Simms in 1985 c. 42 by Scott Brunner in 1983 d. 39 by Jeff Hostetler in 1990

24. Name the Giants nose tackle who knocked Joe Montana out of the 1986 playoff game between the Giants and the San Francisco 49ers.

25. Who was the running back who went into the offensive huddle on third downs during the championship season of 1986? a. Lee Rouson b. Ottis Anderson c. Tony Galbreath d. Rob Carpenter

26. What was the final score of the Giants–Washington Redskins NFC championship game in January 1987? a. Giants 23, Washington 3 b. Giants 30, Washington 3 c. Giants 20, Washington 10 d. Giants 17, Washington 0

27. Name the gutsy Giants receiver who caught a touchdown pass in Super Bowl XXI against the Denver Broncos when the ball bounced off tight end Mark Bavaro's hands in the end zone.

28. Which Giants running back carried the ball 43 times in a game against the Tampa Bay Buccaneers in 1983? a. Joe Morris b. Butch Woolfolk c. Rob Carpenter d. George Adams

29. Which Giant set a team record for touchdowns in a season with 21 in 1985?

30. Name the placekicker who holds the Giants record for field goals in a season with 35.

31. Who was the Giants offensive tackle named as the NFC offensive player of the week following his performance in a 1986 win over the Washington Redskins, 24–14?

32. Which Giants punter holds the team record of 931 punts?

33. Who was voted MVP of Super Bowl XXI? *Phill Sims*

34. Which position did Bill Parcells play in college at Wichita State University? a. Defensive end b. Linebacker c. Center d. Fullback

35. Who was the defensive end who sacked John Elway in the end zone for a safety in Super Bowl XXI? a. Eric Dorsey b. Leonard Marshall c. George Martin d. John Washington

36. What was the Giants' final won-lost record during the strike-shortened season of 1982? a. 5–4 b. 3–6 c. 4–4–1 d. 4–5

37. Which team did fullback Maurice Carthon play for in the USFL? a. The Boston Breakers b. The Philadelphia Stars c. The New Jersey Generals d. The Houston Gamblers

38. Who was nicknamed Toast by his teammates because he was often burned on pass plays yet still led the team in interceptions in 1985 with six?

39. O. J. Anderson was picked up by the Giants from which NFC team?

40. True or False: Bill Parcells never played in a regular season game in the NFL.

41. What is Jumbo Elliott's given name? a. John b. Jim c. Jerry d. Joseph

42. Who was the Giants general manager before George Young?

43. Which coach said, "The Giants may have been the best all-around team we played all year" after beating them 21–0 in a conference playoff game? a. Joe Gibbs, Washington Redskins b. Tom Landry, Dallas Cowboys c. Bill Walsh, San Francisco 49ers d. Mike Ditka, Chicago Bears

Bill Parcells, the driving force behind the Giants' rebirth. (Jerry Pinkus)

44. How many Giants were named to the Pro Bowl game following the 1986 season? a. 7   b. 5   c. 8   d. 10

45. Who was the Giant who scaled the stadium wall at the Meadowlands to join the fans' celebration after the Giants' shutout victory over the Washington Redskins in the NFC championship game? a. William Roberts b. Jim Burt c. Pepper Johnson d. Andy Headen

Jim Burt KO's Joe Montana during the Giants' 1987 playoff romp over the San Francisco 49ers on their way to Super Bowl XXI. (Jerry Pinkus)

46. What was the total number of sacks Lawrence Taylor was credited with in 1986, which stands as the Giants single-season record? a. 21 b. 19 c. 20½ d. 21½

47. How many times has Bill Parcells been named NFL Coach of the Year?

48. Who led the Giants in receptions during their championship season in 1986? a. Lionel Manuel b. Mark Bavaro c. Tony Galbreath d. Phil McConkey

49. Which round of the 1985 NFL draft did the Giants select Mark Bavaro? a. Second b. Fifth c. Fourth d. Eighth

50. Who was the losing head coach in Super Bowl XXI?

51. Name the University of Kentucky running back selected by the Giants in the first round of the 1985 draft who quickly went downhill after a productive rookie season.

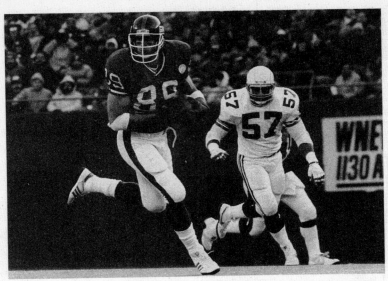

Mark Bavaro lets his All-Pro play do his talking for him. (Jerry Pinkus)

52. What was the site of Super Bowl XXI? a. the Rose Bowl b. Los Angeles Coliseum c. Jack Murphy Stadium in San Diego d. New Orleans Superdome

53. True or False: When Ray Perkins left the Giants he had a career winning record with the team, the first head coach to do so with the Giants since Allie Sherman.

Three of the Greatest

Roosevelt Brown. (New York Giants)

L.T.—Lawrence Taylor, on the prowl. (Jerry Pinkus)

In conjunction with the NFL's 75th anniversary season, a fifteen-member panel of NFL and Pro Football Hall of Fame officials, former players, and members of the media selected an all-time 48-man NFL roster.

Three Giants were named to the squad when the team was announced in August 1994. They were center linebacker Mel Hein, the Giants' greatest iron man from 1931 to 1946; offensive tackle Roosevelt Brown, who played with the Giants from 1953 to 1965 and was a tenacious blocker who would take his place with the defense on goal-line stands; and Lawrence Taylor, number 56, who was with the Giants from 1981 to 1993 and who wrote the book on playing outside linebacker.

REBIRTH AND TRIUMPH: 1981–90

Answers:

1. Rob Carpenter.

2. False—Parcells was an assistant at Army.

3. 1981.

4. George Rogers, the Heisman Trophy winner from the University of South Carolina. The New Orleans Saints had the first overall pick in the 1981 draft and selected the star running back. The Giants had the second overall pick and selected a defensive end from the University of North Carolina named Lawrence Taylor.

5. b. Joe Danelo.

6. d. Perkins returned to coach at his alma mater, the University of Alabama.

7. c. Byron Hunt.

8. b. The Giants beat the Philadelphia Eagles 27–21.

9. d. 1984.

10. Morris—Syracuse; Bavaro—Notre Dame; Martin—Oregon; Banks—Michigan State; Nelson—Iowa State.

11. a. Pat Summerall.

12. Scott Brunner.

13. #53.

14. George Martin, who scored six touchdowns in his career.

15. c. The Los Angeles Raiders.

16. The Detroit Lions.

17. Maurice Carthon.

18. a. 1985, when Joe Morris gained 1,336 yards.

19. Zeke Mowatt.

20. Mark Haynes.

21. d. Bobby Johnson.

22. Eric Schubert.

23. b. 40 by Phil Simms in a game against the Cincinnati Bengals in 1985.

24. Jim Burt.

25. c. Tony Galbreath.

26. d. The Giants won the game, 17–0.

27. Phil McConkey.

28. b. Butch Woolfolk.

29. Joe Morris.

30. Ali Haji-Sheikh in 1983.

31. Brad Benson was the first offensive lineman so honored.

32. Dave Jennings.

33. Phil Simms.

34. b. Linebacker.

35. c. George Martin.

36. d. The Giants finished 4–5.

37. c. The New Jersey Generals.

38. Elvis Patterson.

39. The St. Louis Cardinals.

40. True. Parcells was drafted by the Detroit Lions in the seventh round of the 1964 draft but was released by them before the end of the exhibition season.

41. a. John.

42. Andy Robustelli.

43. d. Mike Ditka, whose Bears beat the Giants 21–0 in an NFC conference playoff game at Soldier Field in Chicago in 1985.

44. c. 8: Mark Bavaro, Brad Benson, Jim Burt, Harry Carson, Sean Landeta, Leonard Marshall, Joe Morris, and Lawrence Taylor.

45. b. Jim Burt.

46. c. 20½.

47. Once, in 1986, by the *Sporting News*.

48. b. Mark Bavaro led the team in receptions with 66.

49. c. Fourth round—the Giants couldn't believe their good fortune when Bavaro was still available in round four, and they quickly selected him.

50. Dan Reeves.

51. George Adams.

52. a. The Rose Bowl.

53. False—Perkins's record with the Giants was 24–35 during his tenure with the team, spanning the years from 1979 through 1982.

5

ON TO SUPER BOWL XXV, AND GOOD-BYE, BILL, HELLO, RAY: 1991–93

Questions:

1. How many replacement player games, aka scab player games, were played during the 1987 strike season?

2. What was the record of the Giants' replacement players?

3. Karl Nelson retired from football in 1987 due to what illness?

4. Name the basketball coach who was a friend of head coach Bill Parcells's when Parcells was an assistant at Army. a. Bobby Knight b. Joe B. Hall c. Eddie Sutton d. Dick Vitale

5. Name the New York Jets receiver who caught the touchdown pass in the final game of the 1988 season that knocked the Giants out of the playoff race.

6. Which kicker beat the New Orleans Saints with a last minute field goal in a 1988 game? a. Matt Bahr b. Raul Allegre c. Paul McFadden d. George Benyola

7. Which position did Ray Handley play in college? a. Running back b. Defensive back c. Punter d. Wide receiver

8. Have the Giants ever played the Jets in back-to-back seasons?

9. True or False: Despite the strike-shortened season of 1987, Joe Morris still gained more than 1,000 yards rushing.

10. What was the Giants won-lost record in the strike season of 1987? a. 7–8 b. 6–9 c. 7–7–1 d. 10–5

11. Which season did Lawrence Taylor miss the first four games of the season due to a drug suspension?

12. Which L.A. Rams receiver caught a 30-yard touchdown pass in overtime to beat the Giants in a 1989 playoff game?

13. Who was named Most Valuable Player of Super Bowl XXV between the Giants and the Buffalo Bills? a. Phil Simms b. Jeff Hostetler c. Lawrence Taylor d. Ottis Anderson

14. True or False: The Giants won their last four games of the 1990 season, which primed them for their playoff run.

15. Which team did Joe Morris join after leaving the Giants in 1991? a. The Cleveland Browns b. The San Diego Chargers c. The Houston Oilers d. The New York Jets

16. What is Bill Parcells's given name?

17. What is former center Bart Oates's profession off the field?

18. Jeff Hostetler left Penn State to play quarterback at which Big East school? a. Boston College b. University of Miami c. Syracuse University d. University of West Virginia

19. Which Giants linebacker made a game-saving goal-line tackle against Bobby Humphrey of the Denver Broncos in a 1989 game at Denver? a. Lawrence Taylor b. Andy Headen c. Gary Reasons d. Steve DeOssie

20. What position on the coaching staff did Ray Handley hold before he succeeded Bill Parcells as head coach? a. Offensive coordinator b. Defensive backs coach c. Offensive backfield coach d. Special teams coach

21. Who was the Buffalo Bills kicker whose field goal attempt sailed wide to the right in the closing seconds of Super Bowl XXV?

22. Match the player with his alma mater:

John "Jumbo" Elliott	Michigan
Ottis Anderson	Brigham Young
Henry Marshall	Miami (Fla.)
Erik Howard	LSU
Bart Oates	Washington State

23. True or False: Ottis Anderson never had a 1,000-yard-rushing season as a Giant.

24. Phil Simms's 1990 season ended with a sprained foot in the 14th game of the season against which AFC team? a. The New England Patriots b. The Buffalo Bills c. The Cincinnati Bengals d. The Seattle Seahawks

25. Name the former Boston College linebacker and long snapper who the Giants picked up from the Dallas Cowboys before the 1989 season.

26. Which NFL team was Bill Parcells an assistant with before he joined the Giants as a defensive coach in 1981? a. The Philadelphia Eagles b. The St. Louis Cardinals c. The Minnesota Vikings d. The New England Patriots

27. Name the Giants wide receiver who was nicknamed the Touchdown Maker?

28. Name the Giants running back who dashed 89 yards for a touchdown on his first carry as a Giant in a 1990 exhibition game.

29. Nose tackle Jim Burt left the Giants to join which team? a. The Detroit Lions b. The Los Angeles Raiders c. The San Francisco 49ers d. The New Orleans Saints

30. Name the former Giants running back who broke many of Walter Payton's rushing records at Jackson State University.

31. Who was the former Giants defensive coordinator who left in 1991 to take the head coaching job of an AFC team?

32. True or False: Bill Parcells won more than 100 games as head coach of the Giants.

33. Who was the Giants placekicker who nailed five field goals against the San Francisco 49ers in the 1990 NFC championship game, including the game winner as time ran out? a. Raul Allegre b. Matt Stover c. Bjorn Nittmo d. Matt Bahr

34. Who was the former Giants tight end playing with the New England Patriots at the time of a reported incident with a female reporter?

Rodney Hampton—the first Giant to rush for 1,000 in four consecutive seasons. (New York Giants)

35. Name the Giant who scored on a 68-yard punt return in the 1990 season opener against the Philadelphia Eagles.

36. Which former New England Patriots head coach served as Ray Handley's defensive coordinator? a. Raymond Berry b. Rod Rust c. Ron Meyer d. Ron Erhardt

37. Who led the Giants defense with 116 tackles in the 1990 championship season? a. Pepper Johnson b. Lawrence Taylor c. Carl Banks d. Leonard Marshall

38. How many consecutive victories did the Giants attain to start the 1990 season? a. 10   b. 11   c. 8   d. 12

39. Joe Morris's younger brother Jamie was a running back for which NFC East team?

40. What is the position former Giants tight end Mark Bavaro's younger brother David plays in the NFL?

41. True or False: Ray Handley got off on the right foot as Giants head coach by winning the season opener in 1991.

42. Name the former Dallas Cowboy who shored up the Giants defensive backfield for the 1990 season.

43. Which team did the Giants beat 31–3 in a 1990 NFC play-off game? a. The Minnesota Vikings b. The Los Angeles Rams c. The Chicago Bears d. The Washington Redskins

44. In week 15 of the 1990 season the Giants and the Buffalo Bills met at Giants Stadium in what would be a preview of Super Bowl XXV. What was the outcome of that game? a. Bills 19, Giants 17   b. Bills 17, Giants 13   c. Giants 14, Bills 13   d. Bills 16, Giants 14

45. 1988 was the final season for two great Giants defenders who retired. Name them.

46. True or False: Rodney Hampton left the University of Georgia for the NFL draft in 1990 before his college eligibility was finished.

47. Fill in the blanks: In the 1990 championship game, the San Francisco 49ers were leading 13–12 with 2:36 left to play in the game when_____knifed through a block and punched the ball loose from Roger Craig, and_____ recovered the fumble for the Giants to set up the winning field goal.

48. Name the third-string Giants quarterback who came off the bench to throw a dramatic 33-yard pass to Stephen Baker with 21 seconds to play, setting up the winning field goal against the New Orleans Saints in a key game in 1988.

49. How many seasons in the 1980s did the Giants make the playoffs? a. 4   b. 5   c. 3   d. 6

50. Which college team was Bill Parcells head coach of? a. Air Force b. Iowa State c. Army d. Rutgers

51. Which team snapped the Giants' 10-game unbeaten streak in 1990? a. The Dallas Cowboys b. The San Francisco 49ers c. The Washington Redskins d. The Philadelphia Eagles

52. Name the site of Super Bowl XXV, between the Giants and the Buffalo Bills.

53. True or False: In Super Bowl XXV, Buffalo controlled the ball for less than 20 minutes.

54. Which Giants defender's tremendous sack of Joe Montana in the 1990 NFC championship game forced Montana out for the remainder of the game with an injury? a. Carl Banks b. Dave Duerson c. Leonard Marshall d. Lawrence Taylor

55. Who said after winning the 1990 NFC championship game, "They keep telling me I can't do it. Well, I'm going to the Super Bowl"? a. Dave Meggett b. Everson Walls c. Ottis Anderson d. Jeff Hostetler

56. Who coached the Tampa Bay Buccaneers from 1987 to 1990? a. Richard Williamson b. Ray Perkins c. Leeman Bennett d. Buddy Ryan

57. For which network was Bill Parcells a studio analyst after he left the Giants in 1990?

L.T.'s Greatest Game

L.T.'s greatest game: Number 56 causing key fumble in 1988 game against the Saints. (Jerry Pinkus)

In 1988, a battered Giants team traveled down to the Louisiana Superdome to do battle with the New Orleans Saints on Sunday night, November 27. The offense was without Phil Simms, who was nursing bruised ribs, and an untested Jeff Hostetler got the starting nod as quarterback against the then 9–4 Saints.

Lawrence Taylor was also hurting that week thanks to a torn deltoid muscle, but L.T. was determined to play despite the excruciating pain, as the Giants desperately needed the win to stay in the hunt for the NFC East crown. Taylor refused to wear a harness that would decrease the pain, fearing it would limit his mobility.

That Sunday night game under the dome was an offensive coordinator's nightmare. Although the Giants didn't give up any touchdowns in the first half, Saints kicker Morten Anderson booted three field goals. The Saints were also battling for a playoff spot, and their aroused defense constantly stuffed the Giants' ball control offense. The lone Giants score came on a long touchdown pass from Jeff Hostetler to Stephen Baker covering 85 yards. At the half the Giants trailed 9–7.

Taylor fired up the Giants defense in the second half despite the horrible pain that often forced him to the bench during the game. He made seven tackles, had three sacks, and forced two fumbles, both recovered by the Giants. He also had numerous quarterback pressures throughout the game. With 21 seconds to play, Paul McFadden kicked the winning 35-yard field goal to give the Giants a crucial 13–12 win.

After the game Bill Parcells complimented his defensive star by saying, "He was great tonight." When asked if the torn shoulder muscle affected him, L.T. joked, "It slows down my backswing."

Lawrence Taylor was voted NFC player of the week for his efforts in that game. It was typical of what Taylor brought to the Giants game after game, season after season. In 14 years in the NFL covering a career of consistently great play, no one ever accused Lawrence Taylor of a cheap shot or showboating after a sack. Many people believe that the Saints game in 1988, given the severity of his injury, might have been L.T.'s greatest.

On to Super Bowl XXV and Good-bye, Bill, Hello, Ray: 1991–93

Answers:

1. Three.

2. 0–3.

3. Hodgkin's disease.

4. a. Bobby Knight.

5. Al Toon.

6. c. Paul McFadden.

7. a. Ray Handley was a running back at Stanford.

8. Yes, in the final game of the 1987 and 1988 seasons.

9. False—Morris gained 658 yards.

10. b. The Giants finished at 6–9.

11. 1988.

12. Willie "Flipper" Anderson.

13. d. Ottis Anderson.

14. False—the Giants lost three of their last four.

15. a. Joe Morris played for the Cleveland Browns in 1991.

16. Duane Charles Parcells.

17. Bart Oates passed the bar and is an attorney.

18. d. West Virginia.

19. c. Gary Reasons.

20. c. Ray Handley was the Giants offensive backfield coach.

21. Scott Norwood.

22. Elliott—Michigan; Anderson—Miami (Fla.); Marshall—LSU; Howard—Washington State; Oates—Brigham Young.

23. False—Ottis Anderson gained 1,023 yards in 1989.

24. b. The Buffalo Bills.

25. Steve DeOssie.

26. d. Parcells was an assistant coach with the New England Patriots in 1980.

27. Stephen Baker.

28. Rodney Hampton.

29. c. The San Francisco 49ers.

30. Lewis Tillman.

31. Bill Belichick.

32. False—Parcells won 77 games as head coach in his eight-year stint with the Giants.

33. d. Matt Bahr.

34. Zeke Mowatt.

35. Dave Meggett.

36. b. Rod Rust.

37. a. Pepper Johnson.

38. a. 10.

39. The Washington Redskins.

40. Linebacker. He played the 1994 season with the New England Patriots.

41. True—the Giants beat the San Francisco 49ers 16–14 at the Meadowlands.

42. Everson Walls.

43. c. The Chicago Bears.

44. b. The Bills won, 17–13.

45. Harry Carson and George Martin.

46. True.

47. Erik Howard, Lawrence Taylor.

48. Jeff Rutledge.

49. b. Five: 1981, 1984, 1985, 1986, and 1989.

50. a. Parcells was head coach of the Air Force Academy, leading the Falcons to a 3–8 record in 1978.

51. d. The Philadelphia Eagles beat the Giants 31–13 in Philadelphia.

52. Tampa Stadium, Tampa, Florida.

53. True—Buffalo's time of possession was 19 minutes and 27 seconds.

54. c. Leonard Marshall.

55. d. Jeff Hostetler.

56. b. Ray Perkins.

57. NBC.

6

GOOD-BYE, RAY, HELLO, DAN: 1993–94

Questions:

1. What was Ray Handley's record in his first season as head coach? *9-8*

2. Who did Mike Sherrard play with before he came to the Giants in 1993? a. The Dallas Cowboys (b.) The San Francisco 49ers c. The Denver Broncos d. The Phoenix Cardinals

3. (True) or False: Rodney Hampton was the first Giants back to have four consecutive 1,000-yard-rushing seasons?

4. Which running back made his NFL debut in the 1992 season opener against the Giants with a 100-yard effort? a. Randy Baldwin, Minnesota b. Eric Bieniemy, San Diego c. Ricky Watters, San Francisco d. Edgar Bennett, Green Bay

5. Who is the Giants' all-time leading scorer? a. Pete Gogolak b. Pat Summerall c. Frank Gifford d. Ken Strong

6. Who was Ray Handley's first choice as quarterback to begin his first season as head coach in 1991?

7. For which team did Dan Reeves play professional football?

8. The lone Giants 1993 playoff win was against which team? a. The Washington Redskins b. The Detroit Lions c. The Green Bay Packers d. The Minnesota Vikings

9. Who led the Giants in sacks in 1991? a. Pepper Johnson b. Lawrence Taylor c. Leonard Marshall d. Corey Miller

10. Which team did Carl Banks sign with in 1993 after leaving the Giants? a. The Washington Redskins b. The Detroit Lions c. The Cleveland Browns d. The Cincinnati Bengals

11. After falling behind 34–0 in this 1992 game, the Giants scored four touchdowns on four consecutive possessions

but came up short 34–28. Who was the team they lost to?
a. The Denver Broncos b. The Dallas Cowboys c. The Phoenix Cardinals d. The Buffalo Bills

12. Which school is Dan Reeves's alma mater? a. University
of Alabama b. University of Colorado c. University of South
Carolina d. University of Pittsburgh

13. His father was a Giants defensive back in the 1950s and
early 1960s, and he is currently Dan Reeves's defensive coordinator. Who is he?

14. Who was the Giants' first-round pick in the 1991 NFL
draft?

15. Which linebacker led the New York Giants in tackles in
1993? a. Corey Miller b. Carlton Bailey c. Michael Brooks
d. Lawrence Taylor

16. True or False: Phil Simms was named to the NFC Pro
Bowl after the 1993 season.

17. In 1992, Rodney Hampton ran for a then-career-high 167
yards in a game against which team? a. The Seattle Seahawks
b. The Indianapolis Colts c. The Atlanta Falcons d. The
Phoenix Cardinals

18. Name the two other candidates who were considered for
the Giants head-coaching job before Dan Reeves was chosen.

19. How many times have the Giants won the NFL championship?

20. What was Ray Handley's record as Giants head coach?

21. Which two members of the Giants' victorious Super Bowl
XXV team played with the Jets in 1993?

22. Name the Giants back whose longest run from scrimmage—51 yards—occurred in the 1993 playoff game against
the Minnesota Vikings.

23. True or False: Dan Reeves has never been on a winning
Super Bowl team as either a player or a coach.

24. Who caught a one-yard touchdown pass from Phil Simms with 1:07 to play in the 1993 season opener, enabling the Giants to beat the Bears in Chicago? a. Jarrod Bunch b. Lewis Tillman c. Ed McCaffrey d. Howard Cross

25. Which Giant threw two passes in 1993, both for touchdowns?

26. Match the player with his alma mater:

Howard Cross	South Carolina
Corey Miller	Duke
Mike Sherrard	Pittsburgh
Keith Hamilton	Alabama
Dave Brown	UCLA

27. Name the sure-handed Giants receiver who led the team in receptions in 1992 with 49 and was later picked up by the San Francisco 49ers after the Giants released him in 1994.

28. The Giants played an exhibition in the summer of 1994 against the San Diego Chargers in which European city? a. Berlin b. Barcelona c. London d. Paris

29. Which member of the Giants' winning Super Bowl team of 1986 ran for Congress?

30. Who filled in most ably for an injured Rodney Hampton by running for 169 yards and two touchdowns in a 21–10 Giants win over the Philadelphia Eagles in a 1993 contest?

31. Who led the Giants in sacks in 1993 with 11½? a. Corey Miller b. Stacey Dillard c. Michael Brooks d. Keith Hamilton

32. Name the two defensive backs the Giants selected in the 1994 NFL draft.

33. Which former Giants player said league commissioner Paul Tagliabue should be tested for drugs after the NFL commissioner commented about the salary cap's effect on that player's career?

34. Where is the Giants training camp located?

35. Name the All-Pro inside linebacker the Giants signed from the Denver Broncos before the 1993 season.

36. This player's 1992 season ended earlier than he would have liked, thus prompting a return for the 1993 season despite original plans to retire. Who is he?

37. Which team scored 34 consecutive points against the Giants in a 1992 defeat of New York, 47–34? a. The Dallas Cowboys b. The Philadelphia Eagles c. The San Francisco 49ers d. The Miami Dolphins

38. Which team have the Giants faced the most times since their inception? a. The Philadelphia Eagles b. The Washington Redskins c. The Chicago Bears d. The Dallas Cowboys

39. This undersized Ivy Leaguer came off the campus at Princeton to win a spot with the Giants in 1994. Who is he?

40. Which team did the Giants hand their worst loss to in 45 years by way of a 41–7 blowout in a 1993 game at this team's home field? a. The Detroit Lions b. The Green Bay Packers c. The Pittsburgh Steelers d. The Washington Redskins

41. Who kicked the game-winning 54-yard field goal with 32 seconds left against the Phoenix Cardinals, making it, at that time, only his third NFL field goal?

42. Which team did the Giants beat in 1993, snapping that ball club's 11-game winning streak against NFC East division teams? a. The Miami Dolphins b. The San Francisco 49ers c. The Los Angeles Raiders d. The Kansas City Chiefs

43. Rodney Hampton rushed for a career-high 173 yards in a 1993 game against which team? a. The Los Angeles Rams b. The Cleveland Browns c. The Indianapolis Colts d. The San Diego Chargers

44. Name the running back who carried the ball 32 times for 168 yards in his team's 16–13 overtime win over the Giants in the final game of the 1993 regular season.

45. Who was the last Giant to lead the NFC in passing?

Phil Simms, a pro's pro. (New York Giants)

46. Who is the Giants' all-time leading rusher?

47. Who is the Giants' all-time leader in touchdowns?

48. True or False: Dan Reeves was voted NFL Coach of the Year in 1993 by the Pro Football Writers of America, the *Associated Press,* the *Sporting News, Pro Football News,* and the Maxwell Club.

49. Which Giant was voted NFC special teams player of the month for November 1993? a. Dave Meggett b. Jesse Armstead c. Corey Widmer d. Aaron Pierce

50. How many times since 1925 have the Giants reached postseason play?

51. How many touchdown passes did Phil Simms retire with?

52. How many times have the Giants led the NFL in fewest points allowed? a. 10 times b. 9 times c. 12 times d. 6 times

53. In the 1994 season opener against the Philadelphia Eagles, Dave Meggett returned a punt for a touchdown, helping the Giants to a 28–23 win. How many times in an NFL game has Dave Meggett returned punts for touchdowns? a. Nine b. Four c. Six d. Five

54. Who caught Dave Brown's first NFL touchdown pass in the season opener against the Philadelphia Eagles? a. Dave Meggett b. Chris Calloway c. Howard Cross d. Kenyon Rasheed

55. Which Pittsburgh Steeler running back gained over 100 yards against the Giants in a 1994 game?

56. The Giants snapped a seven-game losing streak in 1994 against which AFC team? a. The Pittsburgh Steelers b. The Houston Oilers c. The Cleveland Browns d. The Cincinnati Bengals

57. Who was the rookie from Kansas State University who sparkled in the Giants defensive secondary in 1994?

58. How many Giants played in the 1995 Pro Bowl?

59. Lawrence Taylor's jersey, number 56, was retired at halftime in a *Monday Night Football* game against which NFC team? a. The Minnesota Vikings b. The Detroit Lions c. The Dallas Cowboys d. The Philadelphia Eagles

60. How many playoff teams did the Giants beat during the 1994 season?

61. Dave Meggett threw an option pass for a touchdown against which NFC rival in 1994?

62. For which network does former great Phil Simms now work as an analyst?

63. For which network did former great Lawrence Taylor work as an analyst?

64. What was head coach Dan Reeves' preseason prediction for the Giants in 1994? a. Ten wins and six losses b. Nine wins and seven losses c. Twelve wins and four losses d. Three wins and thirteen losses

65. Who was the Giants wide receiver who was called for a controversial taunting penalty in a key loss to the New Orleans Saints in 1994?

GOOD-BYE, RAY, HELLO, DAN: 1993–94

Answers:

1. 8–8.

2. b. The San Francisco 49ers.

3. True.

4. c. Ricky Watters of San Francisco.

5. a. Pete Gogolak.

6. Jeff Hostetler.

7. The Dallas Cowboys, from 1965–72.

8. d. The Giants beat the Minnesota Vikings 17–10 at the Meadowlands.

9. c. Leonard Marshall, with 11 sacks.

10. a. The Washington Redskins.

11. b. The Dallas Cowboys.

12. c. The University of South Carolina.

13. Mike Nolan (his father was Giants defensive back Dick Nolan).

14. Jarrod Bunch, fullback, University of Michigan.

15. Carlton Bailey, with 136 tackles.

16. True, but due to an injury he did not play.

17. d. The Phoenix Cardinals at Giants Stadium.

18. Tom Coughlin and Dave Wannstedt.

19. Six: 1927, 1934, 1938, 1956, 1986, and 1990.

20. 14–18.

21. Leonard Marshall and Steve DeOssie.

22. Rodney Hampton.

23. False—Dan Reeves was a member of two Super Bowl winning teams: in Super Bowl VI he was a player with the Dallas Cowboys, and in Super Bowl XII he was an assistant coach for the Cowboys.

24. a. Jarrod Bunch.

25. Dave Meggett.

26. Cross—Alabama; Miller—South Carolina; Sherrard—UCLA; Hamilton—Pittsburgh; Brown—Duke.

27. Ed McCaffrey.

28. a. Berlin.

29. Phil McConkey.

30. Lewis Tillman.

31. d. Keith Hamilton.

32. Thomas Randolph, a cornerback from Kansas State University, and Jason Sehorn, a safety from USC.

33. Phil Simms.

34. Fairleigh Dickinson University–Madison campus, Madison, New Jersey.

35. Michael Brooks.

36. Lawrence Taylor.

37. b. The Philadelphia Eagles.

38. a. The Philadelphia Eagles. The Giants and the Eagles have played one another 122 times, with the Giants owning a slight edge in the series.

39. Keith Elias.

40. d. The Washington Redskins.

41. Brad Daluiso.

42. a. The Miami Dolphins.

43. c. The Indianapolis Colts.

44. Emmitt Smith.

45. Phil Simms, in 1990.

46. Joe Morris, with 5,296 yards.

47. Frank Gifford, with 78 touchdowns.

48. True.

49. b. Jessie Armstead.

50. 23 times, an NFL record.

51. 199.

52. a. 10 times, an NFL record.

53. d. Five.

54. b. Chris Calloway.

55. Byron "Bam" Morris.

56. b. The Houston Oilers.

57. Thomas Randolph.

58. No New York Giant was selected for the 1995 Pro Bowl.

59. a. The Minnesota Vikings.

60. Two: The Dallas Cowboys and the Cleveland Browns.

61. The Washington Redskins.

62. NBC.

63. TNT.

64. b. Nine wins and seven losses—Reeves was right on the mark.

65. Chris Calloway.

7

So You Think You Know the Giants: 1995–2000

Questions:

1. Name the team Dave Meggett played for prior to 1995?

2. When the Giants dropped Kent Graham days before the kickoff of the 1995 season, they picked up another quarter-back. Who was he? *Tommy Madox*

3. Defensive lineman Erik Howard jumped to what team in 1995?

4. Phil Simms' jersey was retired during halftime of a Monday night game against which team?   a. Patriots   b. Red-skins   c. Cowboys   d. Jets.

5. The G men picked up Robert Harris from what NFC Central team?

6. What was Dan Reeves' preseason prediction for his team in '95?   a. 11–5   b. 9–7   c. 12–4   d. 10–6.

7. He scored four touchdowns in the 1995 season opener against the Giants.

8. Name the former Giant who scored a touchdown for Green Bay in the 1995 win over Giants.

9. The Giants first win of the 1995 season, where Rodney Hampton rushed for 4 touchdowns, was against what NFC team?

10. What Giant scored the winning-overtime touchdown in 1995 against the Cards on a 58-yard pass interception run-back?

11. Rodney Hampton became the all-time Giant ground gain-er in what game of the '95 season?

12. Name the two former Giants who returned to Big Blue so they could retire as Giants in spring of 1996.

13. His 54-yard touchdown return of a Michael Irvin fumble sparked a 20–6 Meadowlands win over the Cowboys. Who is he?

14. Rodney Hampton scored a touchdown in this 1996 game to tie Joe Morris' record of 48 career rushing touchdowns. Hampton scored the touchdown against which AFC East team?

15. This former Giant returned a punt for a touchdown against his former team in the 1996 season finale.

16. This Michigan rookie scored two touchdowns on punt returns for the Giants in the 1996 season.

17. How many 100-yard games did Rodney Hampton have during the 1996 season?

18. True or false: the Giants ranked last in passing offense and total offense during the 1996 season.

19. Name the team Dan Reeves went to after being fired by the Giants.

20. Name the Giants top pick in the 1996 draft.

21. Name the Giant inducted into the Hall of Fame in the summer of 1997.

22. What job did Jim Fassel hold before being hired as head coach for the Giants?

23. What was Fassel's former job with the Giants?

24. For which collegiate team was Jim Fassel head coach before going to the pros? a. Washington State b. New Mexico c. Stanford d. BYU e. Utah

25. Name the rookie defensive back who scored on a 95-yard pass interception against the Philadelphia Eagles in the opening game of the 1997 season.

26. Michael Strahan's alma mater was? a. Michigan State b. Alabama c. Texas Southern d. Grambling e. Morehead State.

27. Charles Way and Tiki Barber played in the same backfield at what ACC college? ~~Howard~~ *Virginia*

28. His touchdown reception in a 1997 overtime game against the Detroit Lions gave the Giants a 26–20 sudden death win. Who was he? a. Amani Toomer b. Chris Calloway c. Aaron Pierce d. Charles Way e. Ike Hilliard.

29. His 18-tackle game highlighted a 20–17 win over Dallas in October of 1997. Who was he? a. Corey Widmer b. Michael Strahan c. Keith Hamilton d. Jessie Armstead e. Corey Miller.

30. After a four-year drought these two Giant defenders were named first team All-Pro for the 1997 season. Who were they? *Micheal Strahan and Armstead*

31. His runback of an interception for a touchdown sparked the Giants 31–24 1998 season opener win against the Redskins. Who was he? a. Jessie Armstead b. Percy Ellsworth c. Phillippi Sparks d. Michael Strahan e. Conrad Hamilton.

32. He took Psychology courses to help understand himself better and improve his play in the 2000 season. a. Jessie Armstead b. Glenn Parker c. Kerry Collins d. Tiki Barber e. Michael Strahan.

33. Who was the first Giant to return a kickoff for a touchdown in a playoff game? a. Harry Newman b. Ron Dixon c. Frank Gifford d. Joe Morrison e. Emlen Tunnell.

34. Kerry Collins tied an NFL Championship Game record by tossing ___5___ touchdown passes in the Giants 41–0 romp over the Minnesota Vikings in the NFC Championship game on January 14, 2001.

35. Name the two Giants who were named to the 2000 Pro Bowl Team. *Ron Stone, Jesse armstead*

36. True or False: Jim Fassel never played pro football.

Running in the Pack: 1995–1999

The G men were armed and loaded for the 1995 season. There was indeed reason for optimism at the Meadowlands as this was a Giants team that had won their last six games in the 1994 season, including the season finale 16–10 win over the defending Super Bowl champion Dallas Cowboys.

The Giants finished 9–7 in 1994 and the Giant faithful saw better things to come. By training camp in 1995, the old familiar names that had anchored the Super Bowl teams of 1986 and 1990 were long gone. Ottis Anderson and Joe Morris had taken off their pads, Lawrence Taylor was waiting on a call from Canton, and Phil Simms held a microphone instead of a football in his right hand.

The 1995 Giants had second year starter Dave Brown at quarterback, and, though the reviews were mixed on the former Duke Blue Devil in his first full year as a starter, it was hoped that like most young quarterbacks he would continue to improve and develop.

The Giants picked up Herschel Walker from the Eagles in the off-season and it was hoped that the thirty-three-year-old, 225-pound running back with sprinter speed would complement Rodney Hampton at running back. The workman, like Hampton, had put together four consecutive one-thousand-yard seasons and it was hoped his fellow Georgia Bulldog would keep enemy defenses on edge and catch the ball coming out of the backfield. Yes, there was reason for optimism. The Giants had gone 3–1 in the pre-season, and even the normally cautious coach, Dan Reeves, saw a playoff spot for his team, as he predicated an 11–5 record.

For the Giants, the 1995 season began on a steamy, late summer night in September of 1995 against none other than the Dallas Cowboys, who the Giants had bested to end the 1994 season. The Giants went into the season opener confident they could deal with the Cowboys. The confidence soon evaporated among Giant players and fans alike as Troy Aikman picked apart the Giant secondary, and running back Emmitt Smith shredded the Giant defense for one of his greatest games. The Cowboys overwhelmed the Giants on that season opening Monday night game for a final score of 35–0.

Unfortunately, things would not soon improve for the Giants as they would lose their next two games against the Kansas City Chiefs and the Green Bay Packers. The Giants would finally finish the season with a dismal 5–11 record.

The offense, led by Dave Brown at quarterback, sputtered badly during the 1995 season, putting more than twenty points on the scoreboard in only five games during the season; and critics felt Dave Brown digressed. Brown ranked 10th in passing among NFC quarterbacks.

Rodney Hampton once again carried the load on offense. The hard-driving running back piled up 1,182 yards during the lackluster 1995 season: the Texas native's fifth consecutive year over a thousand yards, including a 149-yard, four touchdown performance against the New Orleans Saints.

On defense, Michael Strahan, starting his second season at defensive end, shined, leading the team in sacks with 7.5 and had 48 unassisted tackles, a blocked kick, and a pass interception. Phillippi Sparks had a solid year at cornerback, holding his own against some of the most dangerous wide outs in the NFL. Sparks ended the season with 5 picks and 76 tackles.

Giant fans hoped their team would re-arm and come back stronger for the 1996 season. The defense was the backbone of the 1996 Giants. Led by Michael Strahan, Jessie Armstead, and Jason Sehorn (who had five picks in the secondary), the defense drew league-wide raves for their 1996 play.

The Big Blue defense never gave up more than thirty-one points in a game and yielded ten points or less in half a dozen games. Despite the efforts of the defense, the Giants nonetheless finished with their second straight losing season—last in the NFC East with a 6–10 record.

Dave Brown once again ran the Giant offense at quarterback and ranked dead last in the NFC quarterback rankings. Brown threw a dozen touchdown passes, but that stat paled against his twenty interceptions. It was dawning on most Giant fans that Dave Brown was not the "quarterback of the future" they had hoped for.

The strain of carrying an offense without an effective passing attack finally showed on Rodney Hampton, the Giants' all-time rusher ended the season with 827 yards and only one touchdown, his least productive season as a starter.

Giants fans knew that changes were in store and two days after the end of the 1996 season, coach Dan Reeves was fired. Arizona Cardinal Offensive Coordinator Jim Fassel became the Giants fifteenth head coach and Giants followers thought the offensive-minded Fassel would rev up the teams anemic offense.

1997 was to be a rebuilding year for the Giants with new coach Jim Fassel, but thanks to an easy last place schedule, and playing in the now soft NFC East, the Giants went undefeated in their division and finished first in the NFC East, with a 10–5–1 record. The team headed to the playoffs the first time since 1993, when the Giants still had a guy called Simms at quarterback and a guy called Taylor at linebacker.

Jim Fassel brought a reputation as an offensive coach and the Giants opted for Florida wide receiver Ike Hilliard with their pick in the first round in the 1997 draft to juice up their passing attack.

But it was once again the defense that was the heart of this successful 1997 Giants team. The defense limited foes to 17 points or less in 10 games. Rookie Sam Garnes found a home at free safety and, in his first game in the NFL, picked off a pass and returned it 95 yards for a touchdown against the Eagles. Jason Sehorn earned raves as one of the top cornerbacks in the league and Michael Strahan was a terror at defensive end with 14 sacks.

Even the offense picked up from the previous season. Danny Kanell, a second-year pro from Florida State, replaced a struggling Dave Brown at quarterback and turned in a credible performance during the 1997 season, hitting on fifty-three percent of his throws and tossing 11 touchdowns. Chris Calloway led the receiving core with 58 catches and 6 touchdowns. The running attack was by committee with fullback Charles Way bulldozing through enemy defenses for 698 yards followed by Tyrone Wheatley for 583 yards and rookie Tiki Barber with 511 rushing yards. The Virginia rookie was also effective as a receiver coming out of the backfield and hauling in 34 passes in his limited role.

Giant fans could see the improvement in this 10–5–1 team in coach Jim Fassel's maiden year. The Giants were also the youngest ream in the NFL and the Giants' faithful expected a bright future from this team. A few even mentioned "going all the way," but the Giants would first have to beat Dennis Green's Minnesota Vikings first.

The game was played at home and 77,710 filled the Meadowlands to see a game they would never forget. Few in the crowd doubted that the Giants would have their way with the 9–7 Vikings who had barely qualified for a wild card slot.

The Vikings had an old Giants nemesis at quarterback. Big Blue linebackers and defensive lineman frustrated themselves by chasing the scrambling Randall Cunningham all over the field in Cunningham's Eagle days. Cunningham had grown disillusioned with football and sat out the 1996 season, returning to the Vikings in 1997. Injuries to starting quarterback Brad Johnson put Cunningham at quarterback for the tail end of the 1997 season, and he was to face the Giants again.

The Viking defense had been battered by injuries during the season and Dennis Green had to move many of his defensive players to different slots to find some answers.

The Giants drew first blood with a Brad Daluiso field goal and added a second field goal to take a 6–0 lead as the first quarter ended.

The Giant onslaught continued as Danny Kanell found tight end Aaron Pierce in the end zone with a two-yard touchdown strike. With a 13–0 lead in the second quarter against a struggling Minnesota Viking team, most Giant fans thoughts were on who they would meet in the next round of the playoffs.

The Vikings and Giants traded field goals to end the half 19–3 in favor of Big Blue. The Vikings defense stiffened in the third quarter and Leroy Hoard barreled into the endzone from 4 yards out to cut the Giant lead to 19–10.

With a quarter to play, few in Giants Stadium doubted that the Giants would prevail. Once again the Vikings played tough defense, and, throughout the 4th quarter, the Giants and Vikings could only manage a field goal each. With time running out in the game Randall Cunningham caught fire, moving the Vikings down the field. He hit wide receiver Jake Reed with a 30-yard touchdown pass with ninety seconds remaining in the game. The Giants held a 22–20 lead and all knew an onside kick was in the offering.

The Giants put their "hands" team on the field, the Vikings lined up, and as the onside kick bounced in and out of the hands of the usually glue fingered Chris Calloway, a horde of purple and white jumped on the wayward ball, and the Vikings recovered.

Once again Randall Cunningham moved the Norsemen down the field, this time with seconds to go in the game. The Vikings had the ball on the Giant 7-yard line. Eddie Murray trotted onto the field to the roars of seventy-seven thousand Giant fans screaming for a blocked kick. Murray kicked the ball through the uprights and Giants fans everywhere cursed, cried, or sat in the stadium or in front of their TVs in disbelief.

The 1997 season ended on a traumatic note. Giants watchers wondered if and when the young team would rebound. 1998 would supply the answers.

1998 was a mixed bag and the 8–8 won/loss record reflected the highs and lows of the Giants. Danny Kanell inherited the quarterback job after Dave Brown was dumped by the Giants and sent packing to Arizona, but at midseason it dawned on Jim Fassel that Kanell wasn't the answer either . . . enter Kent Graham for his second tour of duty with the Giants. Graham had played well for Jim Fassel when the Giant coach was offensive coordinator at Arizona.

The Giants finished strong with the strong-armed, linebacker-sized quarterback. They were 5–1 down the stretch with Graham and avoided a losing season. The high point of the streak was a Giants 20–16 December 13th win over the Denver Broncos. The Broncos came into the game undefeated as they prepared for their 14th game of the 1998 season. The Giants contained the high powered John Elway. Terrell Davis lead the Bronco offense, but when the final gun went off the Giants defeated the formerly undefeated team—a team destined to be Super Bowl champs that season.

Danny Kanell was dumped after the season, but few felt that Kent Graham would lead the Giants to a title, despite his impressive final six games of the 1998 season. Gary Brown, a pick-up from the Chargers, sparked the running attack. The 230-pound back bowled over defenders enroute to a season that would see him go over a thousand yards, but once again few Giants fans looked upon Brown to lead them to the promised land. The former Penn State star had a history of problems with his weight and a record of erratic performances. The Giant defense, which had been the strong suite of the team throughout the 1990s, began to show signs of wear and tear. Jason Sehorn, the Giants stellar corner, tore up his knee returning a kickoff in an exhibition game. Jessie Armstead was hobbled by ankle problems throughout the season, and, despite the strain of a sub-standard offense, the defensive unit often played heroically. Michael Strahan turned his game on to All-Pro mode with 15 sacks for the season and proved to be a solid run stuffer as well from his left end slot. In the secondary, Percy Ellsworth proved he was a ball-hawking safety, leading the team in interceptions with 5 and bringing two of those picks back for touchdowns.

Giants fans looked at the '98 team and knew changes had to be made, especially on offense. They would soon see those changes.

"They are looking for trouble" one Giant fan remarked

at a midtown watering hole after learning the Giants signed quarterback Kerry Collins to a 16 million-dollar contract with a 5 million-dollar signing bonus. The former Carolina Panther and New Orleans Saint signed with the Giants in February of 1999. The troubled Collins admitted he had past problems with alcohol and in the locker room with teammates.

Collins looked for a new lease on life with the Giants. Jim Fassel admitted that a quarterback battle would loom for the starting job in training camp between the incumbent Kent Graham and Collins. Giants fans hoped that the battle would not disrupt the team, as they wondered who would start when the Giants squared off in the season opener against the Tampa Bay Buccaneers on September 12th.

The Giants beat a tough Buc team on opening day 17–13, thanks to two defensive touchdowns, but showed little offense as Kent Graham hit on 12 of 23 passing for just 91 yards.

The following week the Giants were humiliated 50–21 and the score was a good indication of how inept the Giants looked. The Redskins went into the endzone on their first three possessions with the bulk of the damage being done by running back Stephen Davis, who ran for 126 yards, and quarterback Brad Johnson, who hit on 20 of 28 passes for 231 yards and three touchdowns.

The 50 points given up was the most by the Giants since the 1966 team—perhaps the worst team in Giants history—which had one win in their 14 game season. There would be little for Giant fans to feel good about for the rest of the 1999 season.

Giant fans looked at the 1999 team and sadly shook their collective heads. The team finished 7–9 losing their last three games. Kerry Collins took over the quarterback job from Kent Graham in the final seven games.

Though the Giants finished 2–5 with Collins as a starter, he nonetheless showed an ability to move the offense up and down the field. Collins threw for 240 or more yards in each of his games, and he had two 300-yard games. Collins was the first Giants' quarterback to accomplish that feat since Phil Simms. The wide out duo of Amani Toomer and Ike Hilliard teamed for 151 pass receptions—unheard of stats for Giants receivers—and many Giants fans considered the twosome the most prolific receiving combo since the days of Gifford and Shofner in the early '60s.

The Giant offense was pass orientated mainly due to the fact that the running game was nearly non-existent. Joe Montgomery, a rookie from Ohio State, was the Giants' top rusher with an anemic 348 yards. The team averaged less than a 100 yards rushing—pathetic by NFL standards.

The defense, which often tired late in games because the offense could not sustain drives, seemed to come apart in the second half of the season. The Giants gave up 23 or more points in 7 of the last 8 games of the season.

It didn't take a genius to see changes were needed in Giantland, other than changing the uniform back to the traditional uniform of the '60s (with the NY logo displayed on the side of the Giants helmets and red numbers for the white road uniforms). In April, the Giants drafted the piledriving Heisman Trophy winner Ron Dayne from Wisconsin and Giants fans hoped the New Jersey native would put the pop back in the ground game.

General manager Ernie Acorsi spent the off season retooling the team for the 2000 season and one major area in which he sought improvement was the offensive line. Enter center Dusty Zeigler, a free agent signed from the Bills, veteran tackle Lomas Brown from Cleveland, and fellow tackle Glenn Parker, who also decided to sign with the Giants in the off season and leave Kansas City. All three veterans were slotted for starting jobs.

As spring turned into summer and NFL training camps began to open, Giants fans spoke hopefully of getting a wild card slot into the playoffs. Sceptics saw the Giants no better than 8–8. Some had them bottomed out at 6–10. But the sceptics were in for a surprise. The exhibition season held little promise of what was to come for the 2000 season. The Giants went winless in all four of their pre-season games. Giants fans wondered if the doubters were right about the Giants' chances for 2000 and if the season opener against division foe Arizona might erase or amplify that doubt.

The 2000 Season . . . The Surprise in the Meadowlands

Giants vs. Cardinals 9/3/00

Tiki Barber and rookie Ron Dayne tore apart the Arizona defensive line as the Giants amassed a total of 222 rushing yards against the Cardinals in the season opener. To Giants fans, it seemed that the long-dormant running game was awakening. Tiki Barber enjoyed his best game as a pro as the fourth-year man from Virginia ran for 144 yards on 13 carries, including two highlight film touchdown runs. The Giants defeated the Cardinals at Giant Stadium 21–16, and the running tandem of "Thunder and Lightning" was born.

Giants vs. Eagles 9/10/00

The Giants rumbled down the Turnpike to Veterans Stadium to go head-to-head with a plucky Philadelphia Eagle team that had destroyed the Dallas Cowboys the week before. Giant-Eagle games are known for their ferocity and close scores, but the Giants handled the boys from the city of brotherly love fairly easily as Kerry Collins clicked on 21 of 29 tosses, 15 to the combo of Toomer and Hilliard. Tiki Barber added 96 yards rushing with one touchdown.

On defense the Giants held an Eagle team that ran for 300 yards the previous week to a paltry 56. The Giants dominated on both sides of the ball, controlled the clock for 39 minutes, and put the Eagles away 33–18.

Giants vs. Bears 9/17/00

The Giants took the show on the road again for the third week of the NFL season and took on the Chicago Bears at Soldier Field.

The defense once again stuffed the run by limiting the Bears to 48 yards on 16 carries. The Giants in the meantime piled up 155 yards on the ground with Tiki

Barber and Ron Dayne motoring past a suspect Bear defense and Kerry Collins throwing for 249 yards and a touchdown on 33 throws.

A 3–0 record, with two of those wins against division foes, did wonders for a team that often pointed fingers at one another during the losing 1999 season. To many Giants observers, there seemed to be a rediscovered unity on this Giants team. Not only were two of those three wins over division rivals, but both of those wins came on the road.

Next up for the rejuvenated Giants team were the payroll inflated Washington Redskins—a team who many pro football "experts" picked to represent the NFC in the Super Bowl.

Giants vs. Redskins 9/24/00

The Redskins brought the Giants down to earth as they lost to the Skins 16–6. The Redskins contained the Giants "Thunder and Lightning" ground attack to 93 yards, and, though the Giants stifled the Redskins ground game, quarterback Brad Johnson took advantage of lapses in the Giants defensive backfield to hit old pros Irving Fryar and Andre Reed with touchdown passes.

Giants vs. Titans 10/1/00

The Giants had their noses bloodied and were now heading south to play the AFC champion Tennessee Titans on their home turf, where the Titans had never lost. The Giants continued to struggle as they went 3–2 after being defeated 28–14 by the Titans. The AFC champs controlled the ball for nearly 43 minutes and scored on three of their first four possessions.

The potent Giants running attack was limited to just 24 yards by an aroused Tennessee defense. Once again, the Giants secondary looked vulnerable as quarterback Steve McNair riddled the Giants for 293 passing yards. Giants fans sighed, their heroes, who only two weeks ago looked so invincible, were looking very much like just another Giant team destined to be lost in the pack.

Giants vs. Falcons 10/8/00

The Giant defense rose to the occasion by stopping the Falcons 13–6 in the Georgia Dome. There was woefully little to talk about regarding the Giant offense, but the defense played magnificently.

The Falcons were held to 13 yards rushing on 14 attempts and never mounted much of a passing game either. Jason Sehorn seemed to be rounding into All-Pro form as he picked off an Atlanta throw and defended on 6 other Falcons' tosses.

The Giants' record now stood at 4–2 and the team was tied with the Redskins for first place in the NFC East. But before the Giants could savor the view from the top, they would have to prepare for an old foe.

Giants vs. Cowboys 10/15/00

The Giant defense rose to the occasion again as they held off a desperate Dallas drive in the game's final moments, stopping the Cowboys after a 14-play drive just short of the end zone.

The defense intercepted Troy Aikman five times in this hard-hitting, no-quarter-given contest. On offense, the Giants running game came alive for 203 yards and Ron Dayne enjoyed his first 100-yard game in the NFL. The Wisconsin rookie collected 108 yards on 21 carries and looked like the piledriving tailback that had won the Heisman that past December.

The Giants would now have two weeks off. Their wounded could heal, and the team would regroup and prepare to host the always troublesome Eagles on October 29th.

Giants vs. Eagles 10/29/00

During that two week hiatus, New Yorker's attentions were focused on baseball's League Championship play-offs, and, when the dust cleared, a New York sports dream was realized: The Mets and Yankees would battle it out in a "Subway Series" taken by the Bronx Bombers in five games.

"There were some guys who really did some outstanding things," Jim Fassel said after the Giants 24–7 win over the Eagles. Fassel could have been speaking about a number of Giants: Ron Dayne rampaged for 93 yards; Amani Toomer caught 9 passes for 108 yards and a touchdown. The offensive line, in particular, played well. Tackle Lomas Brown kept NFL pass sack leader Hugh Douglas away from Kerry Collins all day. On defense Fassel praised tackle Keith Hamilton as well as rookies Cornelius Griffin (also at tackle) and Emmanuel McDaniel at cornerback. It was the defensive line that harried Eagle star Donovan McNabb and contained a quickly improving Eagle team to seven points. The Giants now stood at six and two and some Big Blue fans began to think playoffs.

The Yankees had their parade down the Canyon of Heroes in lower Manhattan that Monday, October 30, 2000, but Giants fans still savored the win over Philadelphia the day before.

Giants vs. Browns 11/5/00

At one time it was one of the great rivalries of the NFL. There were names like Otto Grahm and Charlie Conerly, Marion Motley and Frank Gifford, Jimmy Brown and Sam Huff and Y. A. Tittle.

NFL geography is fickle. This storied franchise pulled out of Cleveland and relocated to Baltimore where the Colts once played before they snuck out in the dead of night and moved to Indianapolis. The NFL, in a just move, awarded an expansion team to Cleveland, and the team once again donned their colors and played in the 1999 season.

The Giants entered Cleveland Brown Stadium and tacked on a seventh consecutive loss to the hapless Browns: 24–3. It was the Giants' 4th straight win. Kerry Collins picked apart a porous Cleveland secondary in the second half. Collins hit on 19 of 31 throws for 257 yards and three touchdowns, one to Ike Hilliard and two to Amani Toomer, who in the past two seasons was becoming one of the most dangerous receivers in the league.

The defense once again was awesome, and none more awesome than Michael Strahan. Strahan had his best game of the season. The defensive end made 7 tackles and 2 sacks—a good, solid effort by the hard charging Strahan. Good efforts would be called for the following week, if not excellent efforts. The Giants would do battle with the world champion St. Louis Rams.

Giants vs. Rams 11/12/00

The Rams showed their championship form as they took an early 14–0 lead. Second string quarterback Trent Green threw for four touchdowns as he riddled the Giant defensive backfield. The Giants made it easy for Green and the Ram offense by turning the ball over three times in the game and shortening the field. Even without Marshall Faulk, the Ram running game went over a hundred yards and complimented the aerial attack.

Kerry Collins threw three touchdowns in the losing effort, hitting Ike Hilliard with two of those touchdown strikes. Despite those heroics, the former Penn State star often missed open receivers and threw two picks that led to Ram touchdowns. After the game, coach Fassel sounded an optimistic and perhaps prophetic note saying that the Giants would still play in big games later in the season.

Giants vs. Lions 11/19/00

Charlie Batch, the NFL's lowest rated quarterback made like Joe Montana and hit on 20 of 32 throws for three touchdowns, befuddling the Giant defense. The Giants added to their woes by fumbling three times and by Kerry Collins having a pass intercepted by Lions safety Kurt Schulz. The Lions put up 21 points in the second quarter. Terrible punt coverage also hurt the Giants as Desmond Howard returned Giant punts for 50 and 30 yards in the still pivotal 2nd quarter.

Kerry Collins once again showed a strong arm as he threw for 350 yards and two touchdowns, but most of that yardage and those points came with the game out of reach. The Giants now had lost two straight, with both losses coming at home. The doubters were out and the ugly word "choke" was heard when some Big Blue fans mentioned their heroes' playoff hopes. But a card was about to be played, all the chips were being pushed to the middle of the table, and Jim Fassel was dealing.

Fassel's Challenge:

It happened at the mid-week press conference, after the loss to the Lions, when a steely voiced Jim Fassel issued his challenge to the New York media. "Get off my coaches' backs; get off the players' backs; I'm responsible for the whole thing. OK, I'll take control of the whole thing right now. You get the laser; put it right on my chest; I'll take full responsibility. I'm raising the stakes right now. This is a poker game. I'm shoving my chips to the middle of the table. I'm raising the ante. Anybody wants in, get in; anybody wants out, get out, OK." Then coach Fassel said the words that stirred the hearts and minds of all Giant fans. "This team is going to the playoffs."

The challenge was issued, and, in a few brief moments, Jim Fassel had taken the burden of performance from his players and staff and put it on himself. It remained to be seen if the Giants were up to the challenge. They would face the Cardinals in the desert that Sunday.

Giants vs. Cardinals 11/26/00

Keith Hamilton sparked the defensive unit as the Giants overwhelmed the Cardinals 31–7 at Sun Devil Stadium. Hamilton led the defensive effort with 3 sacks, as the Giants registered a total of 6 sacks, and forced Arizona into three fumbles.

Kerry Collins completed 20 passes for 232 yards and a touchdown, but there were numerous contributors. "Thunder and Lightning" bulldozed and darted through an inept Arizona defense, and a solid offensive line allowed Kerry Collins to move the offense to score in every quarter and team up with his old Penn State teammate, Joe Jurevicius, on a couple of completions.

Giants players had taken coach Fassel's wake up call seriously and next week they would face the Redskins who had bested them in week four of the season. This time they would be playing them on the Redskins' home ground.

Giants vs. Redskins 12/3/00

It was the biggest game the Giants had played in nearly three years and the Giants took sole possession in the NFC East by besting the Redskins in a defensive struggle: 9–7. Playing perhaps their best game of the season, an aroused Giants defense limited the Redskins to 29 yards rushing and swarmed quarterback Brad Johnson, rendering him completely ineffective. Brad Daluiso booted three field goals giving the Giants the victory.

The Giants were now rounding into the main stretch of the season at 9–4, a playoff spot was looking more and more like a reality, and if the Giants could win the final three games against the Steelers, Cowboys (on the road), and the Jaguars, they would not only win the NFC East but would have home field throughout the playoffs. Giant fans shrugged their shoulders, muttered, and grinned: "Who would have thunk it?"

Giants vs. Steelers 12/10/00

"This team was ready to play and went out and played," head coach Jim Fassel said after the Giants took apart the Pittsburgh Steelers at Giants Stadium.

Kerry Collins and Amani Toomer put on a pass and catch clinic as Collins hit on 24 of 35 passes for 333 yards and a pair of touchdowns. Amani Toomer hauled in nine of those throws for 136 yards and a touchdown. Another solid game was played by the offensive line which yielded a lone sack to the Steelers, who dropped to 7–7. The Giants defense contained running back Jerome Bettis and harassed Steeler quarterback Kordell Stewart, simply manhandling a formidable Pittsburgh team.

The Giants were playing their best football of the season, as observers pointed out. Yes, the Giants were indeed hot, and many Giant fans were experiencing a dream that they had not dared to dream in August. There were visions of a Super Bowl dancing in the heads of many Giant fans.

Giants vs. Cowboys 12/17/00

The Giants clinched the NFC East in a nationally televised Sunday night game from Texas Stadium. Trailing 13–0 in the third quarter, the Giants sucked it up, tightened their chinstraps, and went to work.

Although the Giants started all four of their 3rd quarter drives in good field position, they didn't produce any points. Brad Daluiso missed all three of his field goal attempts, and the Giants had nothing to show for their efforts until Kerry Collins found Amani Toomer behind the Cowboy defense and hit him with a 33-yard touchdown pass. After an Emmanuel McDaniel interception set the Giants up on the Cowboys' 17-yard line, Tiki Barber took the ball on a dive play, but instead read Greg Comella's block on Dallas linebacker Dexter Coakley and took the play to the outside, outraced a defensive back, and took the ball in for what would be the lead and the game. Late in the game Brad Daluiso finally found the range. The Giants had a 17–13 lead and that is how it ended.

The Giant defense was once again magnificent. Dallas gained a scant 145 yards for the game—the lowest amount of yards the Giants yielded in a game in 9 years. Future Hall of Famer Emmitt Smith was held to 48 yards on 24 carries.

"This team showed a hell of a lot of mental toughness," Jim Fassel said after the come-from-behind win. One more game remained for the season and a shot at home field advantage throughout the playoffs, but a feisty Jacksonville team would not make it easy.

Giants vs. Jaguars 12/23/00

The Giants trailed 10–7 going into the 4th quarter in a bitter cold game at Giants Stadium, but Kerry Collins ignited the Giant offense with touchdown throws to Ike Hilliard and Amani Toomer, who enjoyed a career day by hooking up on 8 Collins' passes for 193 yards and a crucial 4th quarter score. Collins for the day completed 22 of 39 passes for 321 yards and two touchdowns. Collins and Toomer hooked up on a 54-yard touchdown pass that gave the team a 21–10 lead in the game with 3:05 left.

The Jaguars, however, weren't about to roll over and play dead. Mark Brunell moved the Jags 61 yards on three plays, the big play being a 50-yard pass to Keenan McCardell. Brunnell found former Jet Kyle Brady in the back of the end zone with a 5-yard touchdown throw and moments later found the tight end once again in the end zone with the two point conversion to cut the Giants' lead to 21–18.

The Jags lined up in what even an XFL cheerleader knew would be an onside kick attempt, and in a play that was destined for the highlights tape that week, Jason Sehorn plucked the errant kick out of the air and sprinted 38 yards to the goal line, giving the Giants a 28–18 lead.

With 1:51 left and the Giants holding a ten point lead, Brunell and the Jaguars were still not through. Alvis Whitted took a 12-yard pass from Brunell into the end-zone with 19 seconds to go in the game to make it 28–25 Giants.

Once again Jacksonville attempted an onside kick and once again Jason Sehorn recovered, this time cradling the ball on the ground as time ran out on the Jaguars. The 12–4 Giants would enjoy home field advantage through-out the playoffs. Yep, who would have believed it?

The Playoffs

Giants vs. Eagles 1/7/01

Being the top seed in the NFC, the Giants enjoyed a bye in the first week of the NFL playoffs. The walking wounded healed, and the Giants had an extra week to prepare for their division playoff opponent, the Philadel-phia Eagles.

The Giants went into this playoff game feeling confi-dent, and fans pointed out the Giants "owned" the team ninety miles to the south. There was reason to justify that claim. The Giants had handled the Eagles in both meetings of the past season and had beaten the boys from the city of Brotherly Love nine times in the last four years. More cautious Giant fans pointed to a quickly improving Eagle team with a mobile Donovan McNabb at quarterback. The Eagles were developing a solid offense to go along with their traditionally aggressive defense and had won 7 of their last 8 games, including the wildcard playoff win over the Tampa Bay Buccaneers the week before. The Eagles might be a tough bird for the Giants to carve up.

It had been nearly thirty-five years since a Giant player returned an opening kickoff for a score. Clarence Childs was the last to go all the way with an opening kick against Cleveland in 1966, until Ron Dixon grabbed the opening kickoff against the Eagles and took the ball up the middle for a 97-yard touchdown.

A record crowd of 78,765, the largest to ever see a Giants game in Giants Stadium, saw the Giants defense play superbly. They sacked Donovan McNabb six times, constantly harrying and knocking down the Eagle quarterback. The second year pro out of Syracuse rushed for just 17 yards on 5 carries and his passing stats gave credence to the job the Giants did on defense. McNabb just hit on 20 of 41 throws for only 181 yards.

One of those throws was picked off by Jason Sehorn in a jaw-dropping display of athleticism as McNabb tried to hit Terrance Small and the Giants corner broke on the ball. As Sehorn dived for the ball, he batted it up in the air and while on the ground, the Giant cornerback caught it, got up on his feet, and sprinted 32 yards for the touchdown, making the score 17–0. The Giants had a 17–3 halftime lead and played conservative ball control offense for the rest of the game.

The Giants relied on their defense to contain the Eagles in the second half, holding them to 46 rushing yards for the rest of the game. The Giants controlled the clock for 36 minutes and 9 seconds and when the final gun went off, Big Blue had a 20–10 win. "Our defense was phenomenal," Jim Fassel said after the Giant triumph then added, "I've seen our defense play well at times. But I don't think they have ever gone on the field and just taken over the game like that."

The Giants had indeed stuffed the birds from Philly and had carved them up. But the Giants would need another Herculean effort the following Sunday when the Minnesota Vikings and their potent offensive machine would be coming to the Meadowlands to play the Giants for the NFC championship. The winner would go to the Super Bowl.

Annihilation at the Meadowlands
Giants vs. Vikings 1/14/01

The Giants brought out the legends from their storied past and made the trio honorary captains for the NFC championship game against the Vikings. The record crowd of 79,310 cheered themselves into a frenzy as Ottis Anderson, Harry Carson, and Lawrence Taylor were introduced and took their place at midfield for the coin toss. The Giants won the toss—it was an omen of things to come.

The game plan devised by offensive coordinator Sean Payton called for the Giants to attack the Vikings weak secondary, and attack they did. The Giants took the ball and looked sharp on their opening drive. On the fifth play, Collins found Ike Hilliard streaking downfield and caught him in mid-stride with a 46-yard touchdown pass.

The Vikings fumbled the Giants' kickoff and Big Blue recovered. Collins once again found the open man as he hit fullback Greg Comella, who got behind linebacker Dwayne Rudd and reeled in Collins' throw for an 18-yard touchdown catch. The rout was on and only two minutes and 13 seconds had gone by in the game.

The Giant defense played their best game of the season, if not the decade. Some even said it might have been the finest defensive effort in the 76-year history of the franchise. They completely shut down Minnesota's scoring machine. NFC rushing leader Robert Smith was limited to 44 yards. The All-Pro receiving duo of Randy Moss and Chris Carter, who had run roughshod over NFL defensive backfields, were held to 5 catches for 42 yards. Jason Sehorn once again seemed to be returning to his 1997 All-Pro form, outplaying the dangerous Moss. At the other corner, Dave Thomas dominated the elusive glue-fingered Chris Carter. But once again kudos had to go the defensive line and linebackers who relent-

Team owner Wellington Mara with the George S. Halas trophy after the Giants defeated the Vikings 41–0 in the NFC championship game, January 14, 2001. (Jerry Pinkus)

lessly pressured and harassed 2nd year Vikings quarterback Daunte Culpepper into mistakes. The Pro Bowl bound Culpepper was sacked four times and intercepted three times. The Viking offense was not only shut down, they were shut out. This would prove to be the first time that head coach Dennis Green had ever seen his Vikings go scoreless in an NFL game. If the Giants defense was flawless, the same could be said of Kerry Collins and the Giants offense. Collins tied an NFL record by throwing for five touchdowns against the Vikings. Collins also hit on 28 of 39 throws for 381 yards. "It was the most complete game I've ever played," Collins said after his record-tying performance. The total offensive effort for the Giants was 518 yards to a paltry 114 yards for the Vikings.

The Giants were the champions of the NFC, and, just as the Giants were savoring their win, the Oakland Raiders and the Baltimore Ravens were beginning to battle in Oakland for the right to play the Giants on January 28, 2001, at Super Bowl XXXV in Tampa Bay.

End of the Dream
Super Bowl XXXV: Giants vs. Ravens 1/28/01

It would be Baltimore that the Giants would face in the Super Bowl in Tampa. "Baltimore again" old-time Giant fans muttered bitterly to themselves, remembering the 23–17 sudden death loss to the Baltimore Colts in 1958 at Yankee Stadium, and a year later taking a lead into the 4th quarter against the same Colts, only to lose 31–16 to a team heavy with future Hall of Famers. That Colt team boasted four future Hall of Famers on offense: Jim Parker at tackle, Ray Berry at wide receiver, Lenny Moore at halfback, and the legendary Johnny Unitas at quarterback.

Unlike the current Baltimore Raven team the Giants would face, that Baltimore team was capable of lighting up the scoreboard. The 2000 Ravens had Tampa Bay-castoff Trent Dilfer at quarterback—a strong armed, experienced signal caller who no one would mistake for Johnny Unitas. Running back Jamal Lewis moved the ball for the Ravens. The Tennessee rookie gained 1,364 yards on 309 carries. Tight end Shannon Sharpe was Dilfer's most dependable batterymate. Sharpe latched on to 67 strikes during the 2000 season. But it wasn't the Raven offense that caused coaches sleepless nights—it was their defense.

They were a loud, bombastic, trash-talking lot that pulverized opponents into submission. The heart and soul of the Raven defense was middle linebacker Ray Lewis, a 250-pound tackling machine and the NFL's defensive player of the year. With 340-pound (and that is after a weeks' fast) Tony Siragusa and 331-pound Sam Adams at the tackle positions, running up the middle would be near impossible. The Ravens led the NFL in defense against the run, but the Giants hoped that they could take advantage of a suspect secondary and hoped the offensive line would keep the hard charging Raven lineman and linebackers off of Kerry Collins.

The Giants took the ball to start the game and it was three and out for Big Blue. The Ravens had an equal amount of trouble against the Giants defense, and early on it appeared that this would be a defensive game. Some even joked that this Super Bowl would be the first to go into sudden death tied at 0–0, but Trent Dilfer and Brandon Stokley trashed that scenario.

With 6:51 to go in the first quarter that duo teamed up on a 38-yard touchdown pass. Stokley tore down the middle of the field, split the Giants' coverage, and beat Jason Sehorn who expected deep help from a slow arriving Shaun Williams. Stokley took the ball on the 10 and sprinted into the end zone. The Ravens had the lead and would never lose it. The Giants continued to struggle on offense. The running game went nowhere, except for a couple of scattered draws run by Tiki Barber towards the end of the half, and Kerry Collins was pummeled by a relentless Raven defense.

The Giants' hopes were briefly lifted when Jessie Armstead picked off a Trent Dilfer screen pass and raced 43-yards for what appeared to be a Giant score, but a flag was dropped and Keith Hamilton was called for a hold on Jamal Lewis. The call was at best questionable, and many Giants fans felt that score, were it to have stood, might have given the Giants a bit of a momentum against the Ravens.

The Giants gave their fans some hope in the last drive of the first half. Down by a score of 10–0, Collins moved the team from their own 28 to the Ravens' 29-yard line. But on first down, Collins went deep to Ike Hilliard and the pass was picked off by Chris McAlister in the end zone. Collins would throw a record tying 4 interceptions in Super Bowl XXXV.

The Giants ended the half behind 10–0, and Giants fans hoped Kerry Collins would get the offense on track. However it was Duane Starks, the Raven cornerback, who would crush the Giants' hopes of a comeback. With 3:41 to go in the third quarter, he stepped in front of a Kerry Collins pass and went 49 yards into the end zone to make the score 17–0 Ravens. Giants fans' hearts began to sink, but there would be a very brief spark.

For the second time in three games, Ron Dixon fielded a kickoff and out ran the Ravens to give the Giants their first, and only, score of the game. Super Bowl XXXV now stood at 17–7, and a come from behind win was not out of the question. That is until the very next play when Brad Dalusio kicked off. Jermaine Lewis took the short kick on the 16-yard line and headed up the middle, then veered to his right, and took it all the way for the Ravens—for all intents and purposes the game was over.

The Ravens had made good on their boasts and shut down the Giants offense. Ray Lewis was all over the field knocking down Giants' passes and Giants. The Ravens' middle linebacker was the game's MVP. Jamal Lewis went into the Giants' end zone from 3 yards with 8:45 remaining in the game to make the score 34–7, and that is how it ended.

The Giant offense, which had gained over 500 yards against the Vikings in the NFC Championship game, were held to a season low 152 yards against the dominant Raven defense.

Many Giants players graciously gave the Ravens' defense their due after the game and many other Giants promised themselves that they would strive to return to the Big Show for Super Bowl XXXVI in January 2002.

Giants fans were disappointed by the outcome of Super Bowl XXXV but realized they had gone through a great season with their team. This was a gutsy, hardworking group of young and not so young men that put out one hundred percent effort and never listened to the critics and "experts" that saw them no better than 8–8 in August.

So You Think You Know
the Giants: 1995–2000

Answers:

1. The New England Patriots.

2. Tommy Maddox from the St. Louis Rams.

3. The New York Jets.

4. c. The Dallas Cowboys.

5. The Minnesota Vikings.

6. a. 11–5.

7. Emmitt Smith.

8. Mark Ingram.

9. The New Orleans Saints.

10. Jessie Armstead.

11. Against the Redskins at Washington in a 24–15 win.

12. Bart Oates and Leonard Marshall.

13. Tito Wooten.

14. The Miami Dolphins.

15. Dave Meggett.

16. Amani Toomer.

17. The toll of carrying the Giant offense caught up with Rodney Hampton in 1996 who had no hundred yard games that season.

18. True.

19. The Georgia native returned home to coach the Atlanta Falcons.

20. Cedric Jones, defensive end from the University of Oklahoma.

21. Team owner Wellington Mara.

22. He was offensive coordinator for the Arizona Cardinals.

23. Jim Fassel was quarterback coach for the Giants.

24. e. Utah.

25. Sam Garnes.

26. c. Texas Southern.

27. The University of Virginia.

28. b. Chris Calloway.

29. d. Jessie Armstead.

30. Michael Strahan and Jessie Armstead.

31. d. Michael Strahan.

32. c. Kerry Collins.

33. b. Ron Dixon in 2001 divisional playoff game against the Philadelphia Eagles, won by the Giants 20–10.

34. Five.

35. Guard Ron Stone and linebacker Jessie Armstead.

36. False-Jim Fassel had stints with the Chicago Bears, Houston Oilers and San Diego Chargers. He concluded his playing career as a player/coach with the Hawaii Hawaiians of the World Football League in 1974.

Heroes of the 2000 Season

Jessie Armstead. (Jerry Pinkus)

Jessie Armstead

Jessie Armstead capped off the 2000 season by being named to a fourth consecutive All-Pro team. The 240-pound outside linebacker came up strong with 102 tackles, of which 76 were solo. He was credited with 5 quarterback sacks, picked off a pass during the 2000 season, and played his usual aggressive, intense game in the playoffs.

A Dallas native, Armstead chose to play for the Hurri-

canes at the University of Miami and, along with Giants
teammate Michael Barrow, formed a strong linebacking
tandem on the Hurricanes nationally ranked teams of
the early '90s.

The Giants took Armstead in the 8th round of the 1993
draft and the lowly draft pick showed his mettle early on.
In the 1993 season, Armstead played in all sixteen
games, was named Special Teams MVP three times, and
played in nickel packages, with his playing time in-
creasing throughout the season. He led the team in special teams tackles with thirteen and it was easy to see
that the lowly 8th round pick was earning himself a
starting job at outside linebacker.

Armstead played in all 16 games of the '95 season and
started in two of them. In an overtime game against
Arizona, Armstead intercepted a pass and took it back
58 yards for the score and a Giants' victory.

In 1996 Armstead was penciled in as the starting weak-
side linebacker and repaid the Giants with 114 tackles
and 3 sacks. He would surpass those tackle numbers by
registering 134 tackles in 1997, breaking Lawrence
Taylor's team record of 133 set in 1981. Armstead was
named to his first Pro Bowl that year.

The next two years saw Armstead battle through an
ankle injury in 1998 and a knee injury in 1999, but the
durable Armstead never left the starting lineup and his
fierce, hard-hitting play earned him Pro Bowl selections
for the 1998 and 1999 seasons. Jessie Armstead is married with two young daughters. The All-Pro has formed
a charity basketball team that plays throughout the
New York metropolitan area. Jessie Armstead earned
his Bachelor's Degree in Criminal Justice in three years
from the University of Miami. He was born October 26,
1970 in Dallas, Texas.

Tiki Barber

Born Attiim Kiambu Barber on April 7, 1975 in Roanoke,
Virginia, Tiki Barber enjoyed his breakout year in 2000.
Teaming with Ron Dayne, Barber was the "Lightning" half
of the "Thunder and Lightning" backfield. In the 2000 season, the speedy and elusive Barber went over the thou-

Tiki Barber eludes his foes. (New York Giants)

sand yard mark with 1,006 yards on 213 carries and 7 tallies. The former University of Virginia track star also caught 70 passes for 719 yards coming out of the backfield and returned 39 punts for 332 yards.

Tiki Barber was taken by the Giants in the 2nd round of the 1997 draft and quickly began to pay dividends. He earned himself a starting job and started the first five games of the 1997 season, until a ligament tear took him out of the lineup for four games. Barber, nonetheless, finished his rookie season with 511 yards rushing.

Though Tiki was nudged out of the starting lineup by Gary Brown during the 1998 season, Barber contributed to the Giants by filling in as a third down back and coming out of the backfield to haul in 42 passes for 348 yards—one of them being an 87-yard screen pass from Kent Graham against the Eagles.

Barber continued his role as a third-down back during the 1999 season. He accounted for 1,639 all purpose yards during that 7–9 season, fourth on the All-Time Giants list for all purpose yards. He caught 66 passes during the season, a record for a Giants running back, and caught 13 passes in the season ending loss to Dallas—also a Giant record. It seemed that the Giants found themselves a very competent third down back, but in 2000 Tiki Barber would show the Giants that he was a serious offensive weapon.

At the University of Virginia, Tiki Barber had been a 2nd team All-American and an All-ACC first team back as a senior after rushing for 1,360 yards and 14 touchdowns. Tiki's twin brother and former Virginia teammate, Ronde, is a defensive back for the Tampa Bay Buccaneers. Tiki is married and is pursuing a broadcasting career in the off season.

Kerry Collins

The former Penn State All-American was handed the Giants' starting quarterback job when Kent Graham was sent packing prior to the beginning of the 2000 season. The vote of confidence in Collins paid off for the Giants in the 2000 season when Collins hit 311 of 529 pass attempts for 3,610 yards with 22 touchdowns against only 13 picks.

Collins tied an NFL championship game record when he threw 5 touchdown passes in the 41–0 romp against the Vikings in the 2000 NFC championship game played at Giants Stadium. But it has been a rocky road for the Pennsylvania native.

Kerry Collins is a man who met his demons on and off

Kerry Collins gets some pointers from Coach Fassel. (Jerry Pinkus)

the field and bested them. Collins was one of the golden boys of the NFL in the mid '90s. After his senior season at Penn State, the six foot five Collins was taken in the first round and fifth pick overall by the Carolina Panthers. He soon took over the quarterback job for the Panthers, posting a 7–6 record in his first season as a starter. The wins continued to mount for the Collins led Panthers. With Collins at quarterback the Panthers had a 10–4 record the following season, and Collins posted a very respectable quarterback rating of 79.4.

The second year expansion Panthers lost to the Green Bay Packers for the NFC championship, but Collins threw for 215 yards on 19 completions and a touchdown. During this time, however, the second year pro was battling demons off the field.

Collins would later admit that he was drinking and partying heavily with Panthers and his play would soon reflect that fact. Kerry Collins threw a career high 21 interceptions as the Panthers dropped to a 7–9 mark in 1997. Collins struggled in most of his 13 starts. He continued to struggle for the Panthers during the 1998 season, as Collins bore little resemblance to the quar-

Keith Hamilton ready to pounce on the Eagles offense. (New York Giants)

terback that led the 2nd year expansion team into the NFC championship game against the Packers.

Collins was soon released and signed for the remainder of the 1998 season with the New Orleans Saints. There was little success with the Saints and on a visit to North Carolina, Collins was arrested for driving under the influence. The once golden boy quarterback hit rock bottom.

Kerry Collins decided to turn his life around when he went through an alcohol rehabilitation program. On February 19, 1999, Kerry Collins signed a lucrative free agent contract with the Giants. Since putting on a Giants uniform, Kerry Collins has transformed himself into a winner on and off the field.

Keith Hamilton

This former Pitt Panther enjoyed one of his best seasons since being drafted as a fourth-round pick by the Giants in 1992. Keith Hamilton tallied 57 tackles (43 of them solo) and was also credited with 10.5 quarterback sacks—his highest total since his 11.5 in 1993 when he played defensive end. He attributes his outstanding 2000 season to his off-season workout program with Lomas Brown.

Since joining the Giants in 1992, the Lynchburg, Virginia native has been a force on the defensive line, first playing outside at end then moving inside in 1995 and during his career playing both inside slots on the defensive line. The 300-pound Hamilton returned "home" when he was drafted by the Giants. Keith Hamilton was born May 25, 1971 in Paterson, New Jersey.

Jason Sehorn

The 210-pound cornerback returned to his solid playmaking form in the 2000 season, saving his best effort when he went one-on-one against the NFL's most dangerous receiver, Randy Moss of the Vikings. He held the All-Pro to just 2 catches for 18 yards—an unbelievable effort by the 7th year pro out of USC.

It had been a long way back for Sehorn. After convincing the Giants coaching staff in the preseason of 1998 to allow him to return kickoffs, Sehorn tore his right knee up on his first kickoff return in an exhibition game against the Jets on August 20, 1998. The cornerback was placed on injured reserve for the rest of the season.

After knee reconstruction and rehabilitation, Jason Sehorn returned back to action in the Giants defensive backfield. Because of injuries, a pulled hamstring and a broken left fibula that took him out of the last four games of the season, Sehorn only started ten games in 1999. He was far from his 1997 form that made him one of the best

Jason Sehorn surveys the offense. (New York Giants)

corners in the league, and some doubted if Sehorn would ever be the tough pass defender that he had once been. The 2000 season answered those doubts.

Jason Sehorn was drafted in the second round by the Giants in the 1994 draft, and, by 1996, the cornerback moved into the starting lineup. The California native has been one of the best corners in the NFL since.

An all-around athlete who played basketball, baseball, and participated in track, Sehorn spent two seasons in the minor leagues with the Chicago Cubs farm system. The thirty-year-old Sehorn is the founder of Sehorn's Corner, an organization that aids underprivileged single-parent homes and has raised more than $120,000.

Ron Stone

One of the major areas of improvement for the Super Bowl bound 2000 Giants was the offensive line. The offensive line cleared the way for Tiki Barber and Ron Dayne, and it's fair to say that if "Thunder and Lightning" were born in the Meadowlands, then the players that make up the offensive line were the midwives. The line also gave Kerry Collins the time to put up those prolific passing stats that hadn't been seen since the days of Phil Simms. The offensive line was getting the job done and no one was getting it done better than right guard Ron Stone. The 320-pounder was finally recognized after a distinguished five-year career with the Giants and, along with teammate Jessie Armstead, won a trip to Hawaii to play in the Pro Bowl. The former Boston College star was drafted in 1993 in the fourth round by the Cowboys. Before Stone was shifted over to the offensive line he had been a standout on the Eagles defensive line.

He played in four games for the champion Dallas Cowboys during the 1993 season and continued to play as a spot starter and a reserve for the team. Ron Stone signed with the Giants in March of 1996 and soon moved into a starting slot at right guard and has been there since. Giants fans hope he will be there for a long time.

Michael Strahan

The veteran defensive end enjoyed a fine season in 2000 with 65 tackles (51 of them solo) and 9 quarterback

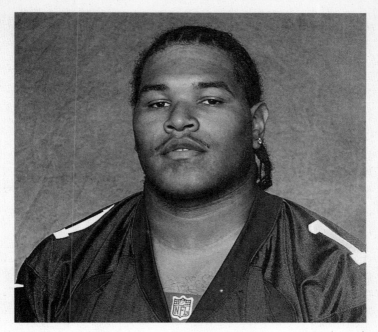

Pro Bowler Ron Stone. (Jerry Pinkus)

sacks. The numbers that reflected Strahan's play in 2000 outmatched his 56 tackles and 5.5 sacks in his Pro Bowl season of 1999.

Michael Anthony Strahan, the son of a career army man, was born November 21, 1971, in Houston, Texas. Strahan played his college ball at Texas Southern University where he registered a career-high 41.5 quarterback sacks and in his senior year was named Black College Defensive Player of the Year.

The Giants took Michael Strahan in the second round of the 1993 draft and by 1994, Strahan found himself a steady job at defensive end for the Giants. In 1995, due to injuries, Strahan moved from right end to left end. His play was steady on some unspectacular Giants teams, but Michael Strahan would soon evolve.

Strahan was a driving force on a rejuvenated Giants playoff team, with 14 sacks, ranking him third in the

#92 on the attack. (Jerry Pinkus)

NFC. Strahan capped the season by being named Giants defensive player of the year and was also named to his first Pro Bowl.

Strahan's ferocious play continued into 1998. His 15 sacks once again led the Giants as he was named Giants MVP and won another invitation to the Pro Bowl. Although he was named to his third consecutive Pro Bowl in 1999, it was not a vintage Strahan year. Slowed by a hyperextended elbow, the hard-charging defender only registered 5.5 sacks and ended up in head coach Jim Fassel's doghouse over his criticism of the Giants offense. Coach Fassel and Strahan ironed out their differences towards the tail end of the 1999 season, and there has been harmony in the Giants camp since.

Amani Toomer

This former Michigan Wolverine has teamed up with Ike Hilliard these past two seasons to give the Giants their most dangerous pass catching duo in generations. In the 2000 season, Toomer latched on to 78 footballs for 7 touchdowns and averaged a very respectable 14 yards per catch.

Since moving into the starting lineup in 1999, Amani Toomer has caught 157 passes. His 79 receptions in 1999 is a Giants record for most receptions in a season. Amani Toomer is a quarterback's dream. With his size (6-3, 202 pounds) and his sure hands, Toomer can go over the middle and make the possession catch. With his speed he can go deep against any secondary. The speedy Toomer has also returned two punts for touchdowns for the Giants, one of which came in the opening game against the Buffalo Bills in 1996 for 87 yards and a Giant record.

The Giants picked the Berkeley, California native in the second round of the 1996 draft after a heralded career at Michigan. Toomer's rookie season was cut short by a knee injury, but he returned back in 1997, caught 16 passes, and returned a punt for a touchdown against the Lions.

By 1998 Toomer was playing as a third and fourth down wide receiver. He caught 27 passes for 5 touchdowns including a memorable touchdown catch that fueled a Giants win late in the 1998 season against the formerly unbeaten Denver Broncos.

Amani Toomer picks up yards after the catch. (New York Giants)

1999 was the break out year for Toomer. His 79 catches were good for 1,183 yards and six touchdowns, and Toomer's performance was one of the bright spots on a struggling Giant offense. At only twenty-six years of age, Giants fans hope to see more stellar seasons from Amani Toomer.

Head coach Jim Fassel. (Jerry Pinkus)

Jim Fassel

With his back to the wall in the 2000 season, it was well known by Giants followers that the head coach had to produce or get out of town. Jim Fassel put all his chips on the table and lead the Giants into the Super Bowl, ensuring his return and another shot at the Super Bowl. In February of 2001, Fassel was inked for a four-year contract to continue as head coach of the Giants.

The day after the loss to the Ravens in Super Bowl XXV, Fassel declared, "Well get back to this game and it ain't going to take ten years like it did last time." With his new contract, the well-traveled Fassel will stay put with the Giants for awhile.

Jim Fassel was born in Anaheim, California on August 31, 1949. At Fullerton Junior College he led them to a national Junior College Championship in 1967. He then went on to play at USC. He was drafted by the Chicago Bears in the seventh round of the 1972 draft and also had stints with the Houston Oilers and the San Diego Chargers as a quarterback.

Jim Fassel launched his coaching career back at Fullerton College in 1973. He gave pro football another shot as a player-coach with the Hawaii Hawaiians of the WFL in 1974. He coached at Utah in 1976, Weber State (1977–1978), and Stanford (1979–1983) where he developed John Elway. Fassel entered the pro ranks in 1984 as offensive coordinator for the New Orleans Breakers of the USFL, then returned to college football to be the head coach of Utah (1984–1989). Fassel came into the NFL as a quarterbacks coach for the Giants in 1991. The following year he became the Giants offensive coordinator. He left the Giants to hook up with the Denver Broncos as their offensive coordinator and assistant head coach during the 1993–1994 seasons. In 1995, Fassel was in Oakland as the Raiders' quarterbacks coach, and, in 1996, was with the Cardinals as their offensive coordinator and quarterbacks coach.

The Giants named Jim Fassel as their fifteenth head coach in January 1997, succeeding Dan Reeves. Going into the 2001 season Fassel's career mark with the Giants stands at 39–28–1.

Giants Record Holders
Over the Years

Individual Records—Career

Rushing Yards	Rodney Hampton, 1990–1997	6,897
Passing Yards	Phil Simms, 1979–93	33,462
Passing Touchdowns	Phil Simms, 1979–93	199
Receptions	Joe Morrison, 1959–72	395
Receiving Yards	Frank Gifford, 1952–64	5,434
Interceptions	Emlen Tunnell, 1948–58	74
Punting Average	Don Chandler, 1956–64	43.8
Punt Return Average	Dave Meggett, 1989–94	10.8
Kickoff Return Average	Rocky Thompson, 1971–72	27.2
Field Goals	Pete Gogolak, 1966–74	126
Touchdowns	Frank Gifford, 1952–64	78
Points	Pete Gogolak, 1966–74	646
Sacks	Lawrence Taylor, 1981–93	132½

Individual Records—Single Season

Rushing Yards	Joe Morris, 1986	1,516
Passing Yards	Phil Simms, 1984	4,004
Passing Touchdowns	Y. A. Tittle, 1963	36
Receptions	Amani Toomer, 1999	79
Receiving Yards	Homer Jones, 1967	1,209
Interceptions	Otto Schnellbacher, 1951	11
	Jim Patton, 1958	11
Punting Average	Don Chandler, 1959	46.6
Punt Return Average	Merle Hapes, 1942	15.5
Kickoff Return Average	John Salscheider, 1949	31.6
Field Goals	Ali Haji-Sheikh, 1983	35
Points	Ali Haji-Sheikh, 1983	127
Touchdowns	Joe Morris, 1985	22
Sacks	Lawrence Taylor, 1986	20½

Individual Records—Single Game

Rushing Yards	Gene "Choo-Choo" Roberts, 11/12/50	218
Passing Yards	Phil Simms, 10/13/85	513
Passing Touchdowns	Y. A. Tittle, 10/28/62	7
Receptions	Tiki Barber, 1/2/2000	13
Receiving Yards	Del Shofner, 10/28/62	269
Interceptions	Many players	3
	Last time by Terry Kinnard, 9/27/87	
Touchdowns	Ron Johnson, 10/2/72	4
	Earnest Gray, 9/7/80	4
	Rodney Hampton, 9/24/1995	4
Field Goals	Joe Danelo, 10/18/81	6
Points	Ron Johnson, 10/2/72	24
	Earnest Gray, 9/7/80	24
	Rodney Hampton, 9/24/1995	24